BASKETS

A Book for Makers and Collectors

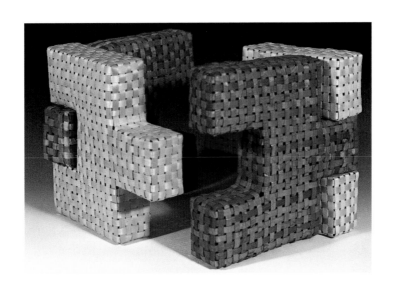

"Baskets have been called the most destructible of all textile constructions. Unlike ceramics, few very ancient baskets have managed to survive. Yet, through the persistence of tradition, through the extreme conservatism which has made basketry virtually changeless, baskets have withstood all the destructive forces to which they are so subject: moisture, heat, fire, mold, insects, wear. Although the life span of an individual basket is very short, another basket takes its place. Baskets have been replaced, over and over and over, unmodified, unimproved, unchanged. So, through the centuries, baskets have shown a remarkable endurance. In their perpetual freshness, they are startling survivals from the past."

Ed Rossbach, **The Nature of Basketry**

BASKETS

A Book for Makers and Collectors

Billie Ruth Sudduth

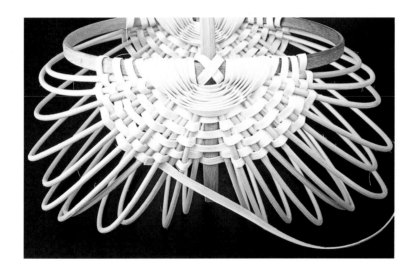

Hand Books Press

MADISON, WISCONSIN U.S.A.

Distributed by North Light Books
CINCINNATI, OHIO U.S.A.

BASKETS
A Book for Makers and Collectors
By Billie Ruth Sudduth

Primary photographer: Robert Chiarito (demonstration photos and baskets)
Primary photographer: Melva Calder (baskets)
Design: Jane Tenenbaum
Editor: Katie Kazan
Editorial Assistants: Robert Winters; Nikki Muenchow

Published by
Hand Books Press, a joint venture of
THE GUILD and Design Books International
931 E. Main Street #106
Madison, WI 53703 USA
TEL 608-256-1990 • TEL 800-969-1556 • FAX 608-256-1938

Distributed by
North Light Books, an imprint of F&W Publications, Inc.
1507 Dana Avenue • Cincinnati, OH 45207
TEL 513-531-2222 • TEL 800-289-0963

Printed in China

ISBN 0-9658248-4-5

Front cover artwork: (top right) Clay Burnette, *Tri-ing Times,* dyed and painted longleaf pine needles, waxed linen, 9"H x 15"W x 15"D; (bottom left) Darryl and Karen Arawjo, nest of oak baskets, $3/4$"Dia to 14"Dia, photo: David Coulter; (bottom center) Herman Guetersloh, *Melody,* dyed reed, double-wall construction, 45"H x 24"Dia, photo: Ray Perez; (center right) Keith and Valerie Raivo, chest, cherry, red elm, red oak, 18"H x 30"W x 20"D, photo: Wayne Torborg; (bottom right) Patti Quinn Hill, *Guinea Hens,* paper, linen, rattan and paint, 4" to 11"H.

Other artwork: (back cover) Billie Ruth Sudduth, *Illusions,* dyed and painted reed, 12"H x 14"W x 14"D, photo: Melva Calder; (half-title page) John McGuire, untitled, black ash and cedar, 12" x 12" x 3$1/2$"; (page 2) Ed Rossbach, *Basket with Indian,* photo: Tom Grotta; (title page) Appalachian egg basket construction, photo: Robert Chiarito.

00 01 02 03 5 4 3 2

Acknowledgments

This book is the culmination of 16 years of weaving, teaching and learning. It would not have been possible without the enduring support of family and friends. First and foremost, I want to thank my husband Doug and sons Mark and Chris. They have tolerated everything from reed splints soaking in the bathtub to eating Thanksgiving dinner out of a Styrofoam box; from scheduling a wedding around a basket exhibit to my absence from a college graduation. Housecleaning and cooking became extinct in my household, indeed arts lost in favor of a new art form. Doug, Mark and Chris are the most incredible, supportive guys on earth!

Heartfelt thanks go to Susan Baldree, who taught me to make that first basket; to Lee Hansley, who gave me my first award; and to Jerry Swan, my first mentor. Thanks to Dr. Larry and Bettes Silver; Dr. John and Sally Myers; and Dr. Chuck and Elaine White, who supported me in the beginning by becoming the first of my collectors. To all my students, past and present, to Piedmont Craftsmen, Penland School, and the North Carolina Arts Council, thank you for your support. Malcolm and Connie MacDonald, when I was feeling overwhelmed with the prospect of embarking on such a project, thank you for encouraging me to stay with it. "From one Southerner to another," thank you Ken Trapp, for

Karyl Sisson, *Bozo III*, coiled old cloth tape measures, polymer, threaded vintage plastic buttons, 6"H x 3¾"Dia, photo: Susan Einstein.

your words of wisdom and humor. Your response to my baskets has made all the difference.

This book would not have been possible without the beautiful photography of Robert Chiarito and Melva Calder. The pictures taken through their eyes capture the essence of basketry.

A very special thank you goes to all the basketmakers who shared their work with me.

Last but not least, thank you Grammie for your whammies, Rob Winters for your editing and Katie Kazan for your guidance.

Contents

Kathleen Dalton, collection of split oak baskets.

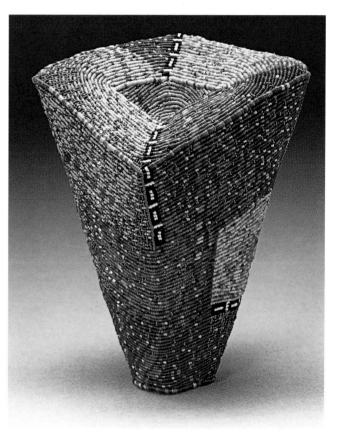

Patti Lechman, *Soma*, knotted nylon, 6½"H x 4"W x 4"D, photo: Beverly Rucker.

Introduction

Within the pages of this book you will find beautiful color photographs of baskets to weave and baskets to collect. Seven distinctive projects using commercially available materials are presented through clear step-by-step instructions and photographs, so that even the beginning basket weaver can quickly get to work. At the same time, a gorgeous portfolio of works by master basket weavers draws the reader through the book, providing inspiration and encouragement with every turn of the page. These artists have mastered and expanded the basic techniques to create their own unique styles.

I have been a collector of baskets for almost 30 years and a weaver for 16. My baskets blend the historical with the present through color, pattern, surface embellishment and form. I am inspired by the classical shapes typical of Shaker and Appalachian baskets, but I look back more than seven centuries for the most profound influence on my work: the Nature Sequence developed by Leonardo of Pisa (Italy, circa 1170-1250). Better known by his nickname, Fibonacci, he was considered the most outstanding mathematician of the Middle Ages. The Fibonacci Sequence is 1, 1, 2, 3, 5, 8, 13, 21, 34, 55, 89, 144, 233, 377, 610, and so on, with the next number in the sequence always obtained by adding the two preceding numbers. After

Billie Ruth Sudduth, *Fibonacci 5*, twill woven basket, 13½"H x 16½"W x 16½"D.

the first few Fibonacci numbers, the ratios of any two progressing numbers approximate the Golden Mean (1:1.618 or 5:8), which has been used to unify design since ancient Greece.

The Golden Mean is found throughout the universe—from the spirals of galaxies to the spirals of seashells. The ratio is found in the spacing of the spirals of flowers, pinecones, pineapples, seashells, buds on a twig, caps on an acorn, and other spiral-shaped objects in nature. It is found in the music of Bela Bartok, the architecture of Frank Lloyd Wright, and the art of Michelangelo, Raphael and Leonardo de Vinci. I use the Golden Ratio and Fibonacci numbers in my baskets. The rhythm of the pattern seems predetermined as if by nature itself.

Chikuho Minoura, *Emergence of New Growth*, 16"H x 21"W x 9"D, photo: Textile Arts Gallery, Santa Fe, New Mexico.

I spent almost 20 years as a school psychologist, where I discovered that I could use the structure of basketry to help students grasp fundamental concepts of mathematics. As Seneca said, art imitates nature, and my baskets—whether viewed as art or craft—demonstrate this idea. Several of the baskets in this book are good examples of the mathematical structure of a natural spiral with its rhythmic, naturally flowing design.

The techniques, patterns and photographs in this book are presented to help you create your own baskets, or understand the techniques of the baskets you collect. Once you learn these techniques, you are limited only by your imagination. Baskets are both visual and tactile. They beckon you to touch, to explore with both your eyes and your hands.

Through this book, I hope you will discover the excitement and the extraordinary possibilities of baskets.

Setting the Stage

Commercially Available Materials

An abundance of basketry materials is available through craft and hobby shops and by mail order. Seagrass is sold by the bundle. Oak, ash, hickory, maple and poplar can be purchased by the strip or by the coil. Reed is usually sold in hanks and coils, priced by the pound. All of these are natural materials from plants, trees and grasses.

Because of its availability, reed is a popular weaving material and is used in the basket projects presented throughout this book. Basket reed comes from the inner core of the rattan palm plant, which is indigenous to Asia and is one of its chief exports. Most reed is grown and processed in Asia, then sent to distributors and in turn to local craft shops.

Increased demand and a dwindling source of supply have dictated higher prices over the past several years, and quality varies considerably. Prices also vary depending on what level of the market you use; material from an importer is significantly less expensive than material purchased through a craft supply house, but minimum orders

Stored reed.

apply. In general, the more you purchase, the lower the unit cost.

Standard sizes of reed range from $^{11}/_{64}$" flat to 1" flat; $^{11}/_{64}$" flat-oval to $^5/_8$" flat-oval; and #000 round to 18 mm round. Other sizes and shapes are available, including half-round and oval/oval. Because it is a natural material, reed varies in thickness, color and flexibility. Reed that is cut in Europe is usually of a higher grade and more consistent in size. While more costly, the quality usually justifies the price.

There are other popular materials for basketry as well, which can add variety to your baskets.

Seagrass
Used to add a soft texture to baskets, this grass is hand-twisted into a cord and sold in one-pound and three-pound coils. Each coil is one continuous length.

Coir
Handmade from the Asian sugar palm, this twisted material is dark brown to black in color and adds texture to baskets.

Vine Rattan
Used to add texture, this has a knotty, uneven appearance similar to grapevine, but it is very flexible when soaked briefly in water. It is available both natural and smoked (dyed a brownish color).

Cane
The outer core of the rattan palm plant (referred to as the peel), cane is shiny in appearance and difficult to dye. It is also less flexible than reed, which is from the inner core of the plant.

Raffia
A shredded coconut palm leaf, this is sold either natural or processed and treated with glycerin and a fire retardant. It can also be purchased dyed in an array of colors.

Commercial materials for basketry, clockwise from lower left: raffia, coir, seagrass, vine rattan, coconut palm fiber; center: waxed linen.

Bryant Holsenbeck, *Bird's Nest Basket*, reed, found and collected objects, random weave, 11"H x 13"W x 6"D.

Above: Collection of handles.

Left: Aaron Yakim, hand-split white oak swing-handled egg basket, 6"H x 9"W x 9"D, photo: Cynthia Taylor.

Waxed Linen

An Irish thread sold in spools in a variety of colors, this is most often used in miniature baskets and in coiling and knotting.

All of the above are available from craft suppliers, and most suppliers' catalogs offer detailed descriptions of their weaving materials. Laminated wood, metal, wire, paper, leather, paper currency, clothespins and ribbon have also found their way into baskets.

HANDLES

Handles are available in an assortment of sizes, shapes, styles and materials. Machine-made handles are abundant and less expensive than their hand-carved counterparts. There is, however, a noticeable difference in quality, with the hand-carved handles being preferable to the machine-made.

Bonnie Gale, fishing creel, buff willow, three-part leather harness, 9"H x 12"W x 7"D, photo: Thomas Brown.

Above: Zoe Morrow, *Five to Five*, woven and shredded money, 6"H x 4"W x 2"D, photo: Charles H. Jenkins.

Right: Betz Salmont, *MI*, 17"H x 8"W x 7"D, handmade paper with interior basket woven with dyed dracaena and jacaranda leaf stems.

Found and Collected Materials

Many basketmakers gather and prepare their own materials, a labor-intensive process which is an art form in itself. As much time can be spent in the preparation of the materials as in the weaving of the basket. In the northeastern United States, ash is cut and pounded. In Appalachia, oak is split. Charleston, South Carolina, is famous for its sweetgrass and palmetto palm leaf. Native American baskets are often made of rivercane and honeysuckle, and in many areas it is possible to gather willow. Kelp and beargrass can be found in the Pacific Northwest. In fact, almost any plant material can be used to weave a basket, including vines, roots, barks, twigs, pine needles and leaves. Many books have been devoted to the preparation of these materials.

A problem facing many basketmakers is the decline in sources of materials. Rivercane and sweetgrass, in particular, are becoming more scarce due to urbanization, development and environmental conditions.

Materials woven into baskets are as varied as the makers themselves. Many basketmakers combine commercially available materials with various found and collected objects.

Tools and Equipment

Basketry is one of the few craft mediums that requires very little in the way of expensive tools and equipment. The hands of a basketmaker are the most important tools. Other tools for weaving with commercially available materials are divided into two groups: necessary and useful.

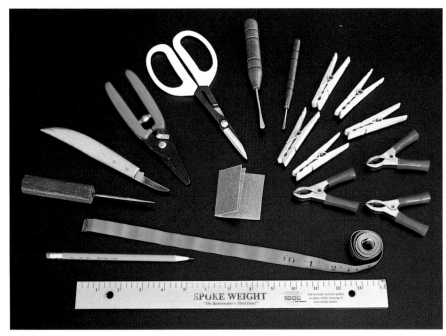

Necessary tools.

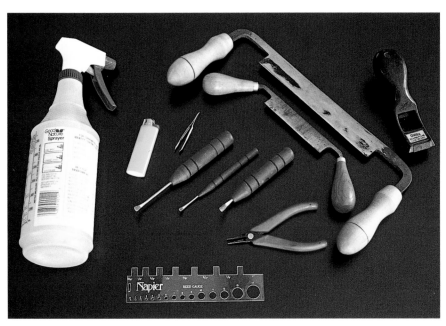

Useful tools.

- spoke weight
- pencil
- measuring tape
- awl
- carving knife
- reed cutters
- scissors
- large flat-tip tool
- small flat-tip tool
- clothespins
- clamps
- sandpaper
- bucket for water

Useful Tools

- spray bottle
- lighter
- tweezers
- bent-tip packing tool
- micro tweezers
- drawknives
- shaver
- reed gauge

Preparation

Commercially available weaving materials, such as reed, require very little preparation unless they are to be dyed. Usually all that is needed is to soak these materials briefly in water to keep them from breaking and to make them flexible. Adding a capful of glycerin to the water will restore moisture to the reed and make it more pliable.

Many opinions exist regarding soaking time and water temperature, ranging from a few minutes in hot water to hours in cold water. A few minutes in tepid water just prior to use are adequate for flat and flat-oval reeds. Tepid water is used because it is more comfortable to the hands. Round reed needs to soak longer as it has a tendency to be more brittle and dry out more quickly. Older reed will also require more soaking time. You can often tell the age of the reed by its color; newer reed is a lighter color and less brittle. Reed is probably never too old to use, as long as the moisture is restored as described above.

Dan Gable, *Tactile Vessel*, masonry nails, brass, melted brass, 8"H x 13"Dia.

Storage

Plastic bags are the enemy of basket reed! Regardless of how dry you think the reeds are, they will mildew if stored in plastic. Paper bags are the material of choice for storage. The bags can be labeled with the size of the material for easy identification. Several bags can be stored together on a shelf or in a cardboard box. Regardless of where they are stored, the reeds should be dry. I find it helpful when working with reed to hang it from a wall hook or dowel, or over a door, so the curls will fall out of the tightly coiled reed. This makes it easier to pull out individual strands for use.

Mary Lee Fulkerson, *Basket Unfolding Joy*, paper splint, plastic, paint, joyful objects, cordage, 18"H x 14 1/2"W x 6"D, photo: Ron Anfinson. This adaptation of the Maori *kete* was taught to the artist by Shereen LaPlantz.

Woven Construction

The terminology for basketry is as varied as the people who make baskets. In most cases, stakes, spokes and ribs are the verticals, while the weavers are the horizontals. "Warps" and "wefts" (terms usually reserved for two-dimensional loom weaving) can also be applied to basketry. The warps in basketry are stakes, spokes and ribs; the wefts are the weavers. However, don't let the terms confuse you. If you understand the technique involved, what you call it does not matter.

In addition to the materials and color, the characteristics that distinguish one basket from another are the overs and unders of the weave. The secret of basketry is rather simple: *over and under*. Of course, this allows for a lot of variation in technique.

Weaving Variations

Plain weave is a simple over-one, under-one weave using flat or flat-oval weavers. It is the most common weave.

Plaiting refers to weaving one flat or flat-oval element over and under another flat or flat-oval element of similar size. The terms "plain

Darryl and Karen Arawjo, *Light Vessel Group*, 3"H x 5"Dia to 11"H x 6"Dia, white oak, nylon, turned rims, photo: David Coulter.

weave" and "plaiting" are often used interchangeably.

Randing is a plain weave using round reed.

Twill weave is weaving over two or more elements at the same time.

An undulating twill occurs when the weavers vary in width throughout the rows of weaving, giving a wavy or undulating appearance.

A reverse twill creates an intentional mistake in order to have the weaving pattern change directions. You do not change the direction in which you are weaving, only the pattern direction.

Diagonal twill plaiting is using the twill woven base spokes to weave the sides of the basket. The stakes are interwoven with themselves, going over two or more elements at the same time.

Top left: Billie Ruth Sudduth, *New Directions*, undulating twill and reverse-twill construction, 14"H x 15"Dia.

Top right: Billie Ruth Sudduth, *Fibonacci 8*, twill and reverse-twill construction, 12"H x 13"Dia.

Below left: Linda Farve, double wall Choctaw basket, diagonal twill plaited, 7"H x 6"Dia.

Below right: Dorothy Chapman, Choctaw basket, natural and dyed rivercane, plaited and twill weave, 7"H x 5½"Dia.

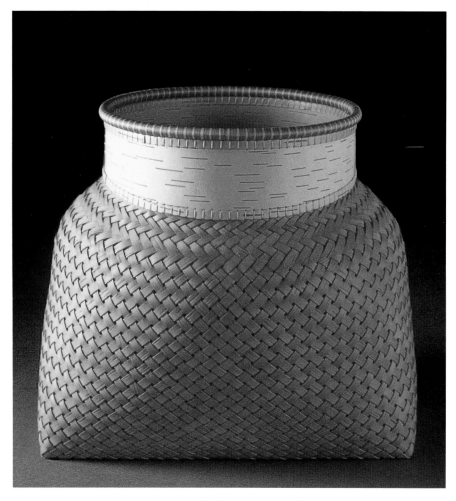

Gail Campbell, *Vessel #291*, white pine bark, copper, raffia, waxed linen, weaving, twining, tapestry techniques, 15"H x 8½"W x 8¾"D.

Dona Look, *Basket #8710*, white birch bark, silk, woven, stitched, partially wrapped, 10¾"H x 12"W x 10"D, photo: Sanderson.

Twining is used to weave around a basket base to secure it before beginning to weave the sides. It is also used to weave the sides of baskets. Twining means weaving with two elements at the same time. It can be done around stakes or spokes, with flat, flat-oval, or round reed. One piece of reed passes in front of the stake or spoke while the other piece passes behind the same stake or spoke. A half twist of the weaver is completed before moving on to the next stake or spoke.

Wales is a technique in which the ends of weavers are individually placed behind three or more consecutive spokes. Weaving can be done in three-rod wale, four-rod wale, and so on. One at a time, each weaver is brought to the front and over two stakes or spokes to the right, then behind the next one. Since three or more weavers are used at the same time, this technique moves quickly.

Weave-and-chase works with two separate weavers or one weaver folded in half. One of the weavers goes over and under around the stakes or spokes one complete revolution, then the other weaver is picked up and follows in the same

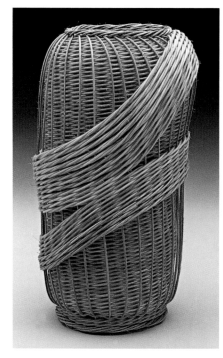

Eva S. Walsh, *Slipping Halo*, double basket, dyed reed, twined, 15"H x 8"W x 8"D, photo: Randall Smith.

Top: Sharon Algozer, *Interconnections I*, reed, yucca, ribbed construction, 15"H x 36"W x 17"D, photo: Michael Honer.

Above: Joanne Wood Peters, *Feathered Crown*, inside-out basket, reed with "feather" embellishments, 10"H x 6"Dia.

Left: John McGuire, *Nantucket Sewing Basket*, cherry bases, cane, oak, ebony, 9"Dia.

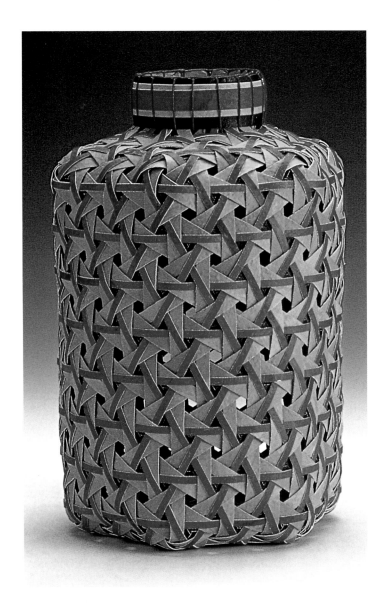

Above: Deborah Wheeler, diagonal plaited basket, reed, cane, bamboo.

Left: Jackie Abrams, *Hexagonal Weave #12*, paper, paint, waxed linen, varnish, hexagonal weave with interlacing, 9"H x 6"Dia, photo: Greg Hubbard.

direction around the basket. When the starting point is reached, the second weaver is dropped and the first weaver is picked up again as the weaving continues.

Bases

Before beginning to weave a basket, you must first determine how you will construct the frame or skeleton. Most baskets begin with the weaving of a base.

Staked base is the method of construction used to obtain a square or rectangular shape on the bottom of the basket.

Plain or plaited is a simple over-one, under-one weave with open spaces between the stakes.

Diagonal plaited is a method in which the stakes interweave with themselves, one by one, forming both the base and the sides of the basket. There are usually spaces between the stakes.

Twill plaited bases have the vertical stakes passing over the horizontal stakes two or more at a time. A commonly used twill base is the herringbone. The base is tightly woven with no spaces between the stakes.

Diagonal twill plaited is a technique in which the stakes interweave with themselves, passing over two or more stakes at a time, forming both the base and the sides of the basket. This base is also tightly woven with no spaces between the stakes.

Spoked bases are usually round. The baskets are probably so-named because the spokes of the basket resemble the spokes of a wheel.

A single-bottom spoked basket has the spokes arranged in a circle, pinwheel fashion. These bases are usually twined or woven in a weave-and-chase technique. A plain or randing weave can also be used. Weaving techniques for the sides will vary.

A false double-bottom basket has the spokes laid out in a pinwheel fashion, then woven or twined for several rows. Secondary or new spokes are placed between each existing spoke and twined or woven into place.

A double-bottom basket has two separate bases woven. Base two is placed on top of base one. The bases are then woven together with the spokes from base two fitting between the spokes of base one. Twining is the technique of choice for weaving the two bases together.

A wood base has the spokes inserted into a small groove in a round or oval piece of wood. Weaving begins at this point and continues up the sides of the basket.

The manner in which you construct the base of your basket will influence the technique you choose to weave the sides. Many baskets are woven with a variety of weaving techniques.

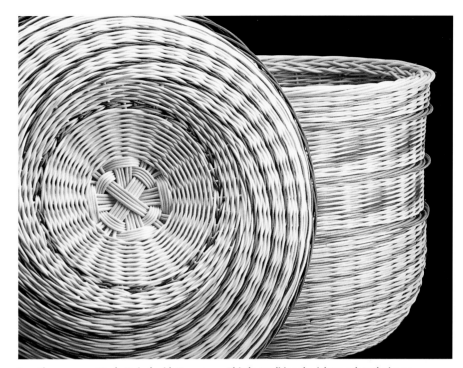

Lee Zimmerman, *Teale Spiral with Tennessee Thistle*, traditional wickerwork techniques, 11"H x 18"Dia, photo: David Lutrell.

Kari Lønning, *Path to My Garden*, dyed rattan reed, double-wall construction, hidden inner chamber with two seed pods, 4½"H x 17½"Dia.

Ribs

Instead of a base, some baskets use a ribbed construction, which probably offers the most possibilities of the conventional basket forms. Two or more hoops are lashed together to form the frame into which ribs are inserted before weaving begins. Ribs can be round or flat. Small baskets usually only require one set of primary ribs. Larger pieces will require additional ribs to be inserted as the basket is woven. Sets of secondary ribs may need to be inserted several times before the basket is completed. Additional ribs will add strength to the basket.

Once the ribs are inserted, the weaving technique is usually a plain weave. If only one hoop is used to construct the frame, ribs are used instead of a second hoop and are lashed into place before the primary ribs are inserted.

> **TIP**
>
> Never leave more than an inch of space between ribs.

> **TIP**
>
> To vary the shape of a ribbed basket, increase or decrease the length of the ribs.

Random Weave

This refers to a type of construction in which no pattern or order is followed. It is difficult to distinguish where the weaving begins and ends once the basket is completed. Weaving is done in an over-and-under fashion to hold the elements together, but in no particular order.

Cindy Luna, random weave basket, metal.

Ferne Jacobs, *Heart Fan*, waxed linen thread, coiled and twined, 13"H x 13½"W x 5½"D, photo: Susan Einstein.

Basic Techniques

Once the variations of woven construction are learned, there are several basic techniques that apply to many types of baskets, regardless of how they are constructed. These techniques include adding weavers, upsetting, carving rims, and lashing. Helpful hints in this chapter and throughout this book make weaving more enjoyable and baskets more aesthetically pleasing. Not all baskets use all of these techniques, but most use some of them.

Most weaving techniques can be separated into stop-and-start weaving or continuous weaving.

Stop-and-Start Weave

Stop-and-start weaving proceeds around the basket one row at a time. Each row is woven separately. To prevent a seamed or stacked appearance, alternate your rows, beginning each new row from side to side.

The beginning of the weaver is placed behind a stake or spoke. Do not begin weaving a row at the corner stake or spoke. By beginning each row in the middle of a long side of the basket, the tension of the weave is better controlled. The weaving progresses around the basket until the starting point is

Jayne Hare Dane, stack of three "covered" baskets, hand-pounded, dyed, split black ash, 16"H x 12"W x 9"D.

reached. The end of the weaver is then cut and tucked behind either the second or fourth stake or spoke past the starting point. The stakes or spokes will hide each loose end of the weavers to keep them from being visible on the inside or the outside of the basket. This technique is called *losing your weaver* and is also used with continuous weaving.

Stop-and-start weaving allows you to use different widths, sizes and colors from one row to another. You can weave over and under one or more elements at a time.

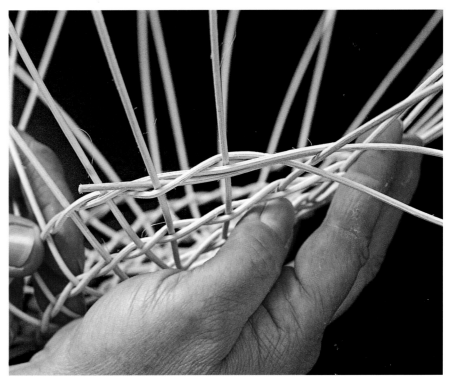

Adding on a round weaver.

Continuous Weave

Continuous weave means using the same piece of weaver for as many rows as possible until a new weaver needs to be added. Continuous weave can be done on either an even or an odd number of stakes or spokes. To weave continuously on an even number of stakes or spokes, an intentional mistake has to be created in the pattern of the weave, or a step-up twill has to be used. The mistake is called a *signature* as it spirals up the basket, moving over one stake or spoke each row. It occurs once on each row when the weaving pattern of over-one, under-one is interrupted and the weaver passes over two stakes or spokes. A signature is created when the weave is plain or plaited and the weave continuous.

A *step-up twill* occurs when the pattern of the weave moves one

stake or spoke to the right or to the left at each row. Again, this is a spiral pattern, but the weaving pattern is not interrupted.

One extra stake may be inserted at a corner to use a continuous weave, or a stake or spoke may be split in two. This provides an odd number of stakes or spokes so that creating a signature or step-up twill is not necessary.

ADDING A WEAVER

Flat Reed

Flat reed has a smooth side and a rough side. These are called the *good side* and *bad side* of the weaver. The rough side will be more hairy and tend to splinter. Always check to see that the good side of the reed is facing the outside of the basket when adding a weaver. When working with flat-

oval reed, the oval side will face the outside of the basket, or, in the case of rims, will be the side that is facing away from the basket.

A lighter can be used to very carefully singe away the fuzz on baskets. Do this only on a damp basket and take extreme care to avoid burning or smoking up the basket.

When a flat-reed weaver runs out, lay the end of the new weaver on top of the end of the existing weaver and overlap for either two or four spokes, remembering to hide the ends behind the stakes or spokes. Pick up the new weaver and continue the weaving pattern as if the weaver were the original.

Round Reed

Round reed is added differently depending on the type of the weave. For plain, plaited, twill and wales, the end of the weaver can simply

Alice Ogden, bushel basket and 1¹⁄₂ bushel basket, black ash, white oak handles, 15"H x 22"Dia, 12"H x 20"Dia, photo: Charley Fryebury.

Upsetting the basket.

lay behind a spoke. There is no need to overlap because the weaver will not pull out once the rows are packed against each other.

When twining a basket, the weavers should overlap. When one twining weaver ends, lay the end of a new weaver beside the end of the original one and twine with both the old and new for three or four stakes or spokes.

When adding a round weaver to a flat base, tuck the end of the old and the beginning of the new weaver along a spoke on the inside of the basket under previous rows of twining. This will secure the ends and prevent them from pulling out. Always place the beginning and ending of the weavers on the inside of the basket.

Upsetting

Upsetting is a technique to turn the sides of the basket upright from the base. Another word for upsetting is upstaking. When a basket is twined around the base, the area along the twining line is where the basket is upsett. The stakes or spokes are creased across the twining line and pressed firmly against the base of the basket. The stakes or spokes are bent over against themselves. Make sure the stakes are damp before bending them.

Bending and Tucking

Bending and tucking is the process used to hide and secure the tops of stakes or spokes before lashing a rim. On most baskets, the stakes or spokes that end on the inside of the basket are cut off even with the top row of weaving. The stakes or spokes that end on the outside of the basket are bent over the top row of weaving, then tucked under the third row of weaving on the inside of the basket. To avoid cutting too much, make a pencil mark where the stake or spoke on the inside of the basket meets the last row of weaving. Proceed around the basket and cut off the stakes or spokes at the pencil mark. Make sure only the stakes or spokes on the inside of the basket are cut.

Briefly soak the remaining stakes or spokes, then bend them over the top row of weaving. Mark with a pencil where the stake or spoke meets the third row of weaving on the inside of the basket. Cut slightly below this pencil mark and tuck the end under the third row of weaving. By using this technique,

Inside stakes cut even with the top row of weaving.

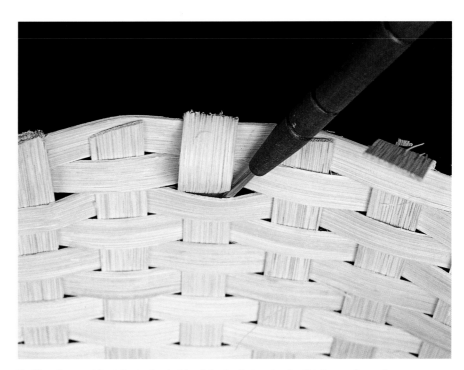

Tucking the outside stake to the inside of the basket under the third row of weaving.

Carving a rim.

Inserting lashing along a spoke on the inside of the basket between rim pieces.

Rim lashing.

loose ends will not show on the inside or the outside of the basket. When creased, dampened spokes will crack and split, but it is unlikely they will break.

Some baskets, such as the *Penland Pottery Basket* in Chapter 7, require that all stakes or spokes be bent over the top row of weaving and tucked to the inside of the basket.

Carving and Attaching a Rim

Attaching a rim to a basket is a technique that gives the basket added strength and a finished look. It also holds all the elements in place. Without a rim, a basket would probably unravel over time. Flat or flat-oval reeds are materials often used for the rim. Some basketmakers prefer half-round reed for rims. This material is more difficult to carve and scarf down because it is so thick, but the finished look is well worth the effort. Using reed of this shape makes it unnecessary to add a rim filler to hide the top edge of the basket.

TIP

Choose reed the next size up from the last row of weaving for the rim material. This allows room to insert a rim filler. It also covers the loose ends at the top of the basket where the bending and tucking occurred.

Lay a piece of the rim material around the inside and outside top rows of the basket and secure with clothespins. Cut the rim about two inches longer than the distance around the top of the basket to allow for overlap. Since rim material is usually thicker than the weaver, the ends that overlap should be carved (scarfed) to half their normal thickness. This is best accomplished by using a carving knife.

When using flat or flat-oval reed, begin and end the rims on a long side of the basket, never at the corners or handle. The inside rim should overlap on the opposite side of the basket from the outside rim. This will prevent an obvious bulge at the top.

When working with half-round reed, the placement of the rims is slightly different. Place the inside and outside overlapped rims near, but not on top of, each other.

RIM FILLERS

A rim filler can be placed between the rims of flat and flat-oval reed to further hide the top edge of the basket before lashing. Round reed and seagrass are frequently used for this. When half-round reeds are lashed together, there is very little space left between the rounded rim, so rim fillers are not usually used.

LASHING

Lashing is the technique that holds the two rim pieces together. It can be done with any size reed that will fit between the spokes, most often $3/16$" flat, $1/4$" flat, or $11/64$" flat-oval. Begin the lashing away from seams and handles. The easiest way to lash is to insert the end of the lashing between the rim pieces and secure it under a row of weaving on the inside of the basket. It will lay along a spoke out of sight.

Working from the outside of the basket, bring the lashing across the rim and underneath it, between the next two stakes or spokes. Use an awl or small flat-tip tool to open a space underneath the rim for the lashing to pass through. Continue moving around the basket, over and under the rim, between the next two stakes or spokes until the starting point is reached. The end is tucked between the rims along

Keith and Valerie Raivo, chest, cherry, red elm, red oak, 18"H x 30"W x 20"D, photo: Wayne Torborg.

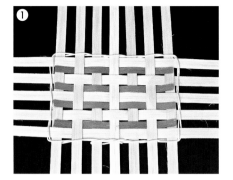

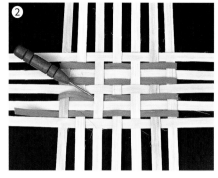

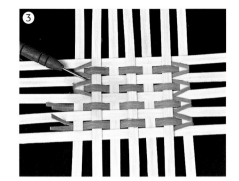

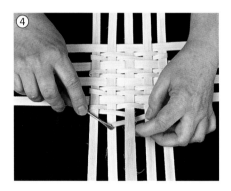

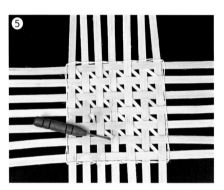

1 Plain.
2 Turned back.
3 Crow's feet.
4 Chain lock.
5 Diagonal.

the same stake or spoke as the beginning piece. The ends will be secured under a row of weaving inside the basket.

Filling in a Base

Square or rectangular bases often have open spaces between the stakes. There are several ways of filling in a base; the following are the most frequently used:

The *plain* technique involves weaving a filler over and under the vertical stakes, between the horizontal stakes. The ends of the filler lay on top of the base stakes and are visible on the inside of the basket. This technique can be done once the basket is complete. Fillers can be inserted between the vertical stakes, over and under the horizontal stakes, but more fillers are needed if inserted in this direction.

The *turned back* technique involves filling in between stakes as the base is being woven. Fillers are woven between either the vertical or horizontal stakes and then turned back to the inside of the base and tucked under the first available stake. The ends of the filler are not visible. The base is usually twined after the filler strips are inserted.

Crow's feet can be woven either vertically or horizontally as the base is being woven. These fillers are cut a few inches longer than the measurement of the base. They are woven over and under across the base between the vertical (or horizontal) stakes. After the base is woven, the fillers are then turned back to the outside of the base. Before the ends are tucked under the first available stake, they are split to the edge of the base. Half of the split filler tucks under the stake to the right and the other half tucks under the stake to the left. This technique gives the appearance of crow's feet. It is striking when woven in a contrasting color from the base stakes. Since crow's feet will hold the base together, twining is optional.

A *chain lock* is woven as the base is being laid out. The horizontal stakes are laid out to the correct width. A vertical stake is then woven under one, over one across the base. Before inserting another vertical stake, a filler is woven on ei-

Elizabeth Geisler, tapestry sewing basket, cherry, sliced agate with petosky stone, cane, waxed linen, reed, palm inflorescence, Mylar-coated cord, oak rims, brass Escutcheon pin fastenings, leather hinges, hasp with bone peg, oak handle with bone fittings, 7"H x 12"Dia, photo: Steve Meltzer.

ther side of the existing stake in an over-and-under weave. Rather than going over the edge of the base and tucking under a stake, the filler meets itself on the second round of weaving and tucks into itself. The base can be twined after the fillers are inserted, although the chain lock will hold the base in place.

A *diagonal* filler does not fill the spaces but is a decorative accent on the base of the basket. Strips smaller than the base stakes are woven over and under diagonally across the base. They can be woven diagonally from one corner to another or diagonally across each corner. The filler strips are usually inserted after the basket is complete.

Above: Polly Adams Sutton, *Sweetgrass with Yellow Cedar*, sweetgrass, red and yellow cedar bark, twined, 7"H x 5"W x 3"D, photo: Bill Wickett.

Right: Hisako Sekijima, untitled basket, kudzu vine, 17¼"H x 6¾"W x 6¾"D.

Michael Davis, *Flower Series—Yellow Dahlia in Blossom*, twined reed, acrylic and enamel paint, quilting pins, plexiglass base, 19"H x 28"W x 28"D, photo: Deloye Burrell, courtesy of Connell Gallery, Atlanta, Georgia.

Dyes and Dyeing

S ooner or later, almost every basketmaker wants to experiment with color. Sources for dyes are as close as your kitchen cupboard and your own backyard. Anything that will stain your kitchen sink will make a beautiful dye for a basket. Weaving materials may be dyed before beginning construction, or the entire basket may be dyed upon completion.

Equipment

Equipment needs will vary depending on the types of dyes being used. Dyes using cold water require little more than a plastic bucket, protective gloves, a strainer and a stirrer. Hot-water dyes need a non-porous kettle made of glass, enameled steel or stainless steel. Avoid using copper, aluminum or cast-iron pots because these metals react with dyes and interfere with dyeing. A stove or hot plate is necessary if the dyebath solutions have to be heated. Tongs are helpful for removing the dyed materials from the dyebath. Dyeing can be messy, so keep plenty of newspaper on hand to cover surfaces before beginning the dyeing process. Clean-up of dyepots can be accomplished with bleach or a household cleanser.

John Skau, grouping of baskets from *Swollen Plane Series*, double weave, twill and point twills, birch, maple, wood dye, varnish, 30"H x 30"W x 10"D.

Safety Precautions

Enough cannot be said on the subject of safety. Although more and more commercial dyes have become available, safety issues have not been given appropriate attention. Natural dyes can pose as much of a health risk as chemical dyes.

Always use common sense and safety precautions when working with dyes. Wear a dust mask or respirator to avoid breathing the dust particles and work in a well-ventilated area to avoid breathing the fumes. Wear protective clothing and rubber gloves to prevent contact of dyes with skin. Keep all dyes and dyebaths away from children and pets.

Avoid making dyes in the same areas where food is prepared. If you can't avoid this, cover all work surfaces with newspaper, make sure no food is near or exposed to the fumes or dust, and do not use the same utensils for cooking as you use for making dyes. Make sure to dispose of dyes properly and be sure not to store them where they can be mistaken for foods or beverages.

When working with natural or chemical dyes, it is important to know if the dye is lightfast and colorfast. Lightfast means that the dye will not fade when exposed to ordinary light conditions. Because basketry material is usually a cellulose fiber, it is relatively easy to dye. However, dyes do not penetrate the fibers; they only coat them. Like any fine fiber, dyed basketry materials will fade when exposed to direct sources of light over long periods of time. Chemical dyes are usually more lightfast than natural dyes. They are also more colorfast, meaning the colors won't fade or bleed onto the other fibers or your hands. Chemical dyes are made for fibers such as cotton, wool and silk.

Reed being removed from a dyebath.

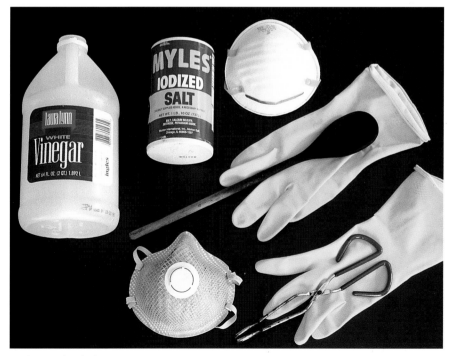

Equipment for dyeing.

Lee Zimmerman, *Night Lights Series*, Japanese weave, three-, four-, and five-rod wale, rattan reed, natural fiber-reactive dyes, photo: David Lutrell.

Only a few brands have been developed specifically for basketry. These dyes are safer to use, but they will fade more quickly.

Variables in the success of dyeing include:

- the type of dye being used
- the amount of dye
- the water temperature
- the length of time in the dyebath
- the source of water (chlorinated water produces less desirable results than untreated water)

Natural and chemical dyes work best when a mordant is added to the dyebath. A mordant is any substance used to fix the dye or make it more permanent, acting as the glue that bonds the color to the material.

Natural Dyes

Until the mid-1800s, all dyes were natural. The term "natural dye" means that the dye color has come from plants, animals, insects or minerals. "Vegetable dye" is the term given to dyes derived from plants. Many natural dyes, such as indigo, madder root and cochineal insects, are available commercially. While it is fun to explore all the possibilities of natural dyes, they are not as colorfast as chemical dyes, nor are they faster or easier to use.

WALNUT HULL DYE

The natural dye most commonly used by basketmakers is crushed walnut hulls. If the hulls are gathered in the autumn when the walnuts first fall and then stored over the winter, the hull will completely dry out and become powder-like in consistency. (Hulls that have been aged will make a richer dye than those that have recently fallen.)

To make a walnut hull dye, fill a 20-gallon rubber garbage can partially full of water and place it in a shady location. Add a zippered pillowcase full of dried walnuts, hull and all, to the can of water and cover it with a tight-fitting lid. Let the solution steep for several days to several weeks, depending on the depth of color you want. Stir frequently during this time period and use a strainer to remove any debris that rises to the top of the can. To mask the unpleasant odor of the walnut vat as it sits over

Clay Burnette, *One Crazy Quilt*, longleaf pine needles, waxed linen, glass seed beads, dyed and painted, 5½"H x 5"W x 16"L, photo: George Fulton.

time, add vanilla flavoring to the dyebath. Once the depth of color has been obtained, remove the pillowcase of walnuts. This will help the dye solution last longer. Crushing and/or boiling the walnuts before putting them in the case will produce color more quickly. Doing this, however, will shorten the length of time the dye will be usable.

Once the dye has reached a certain color, usually after a month, it will not become any darker. The only thing that will produce a darker color will be the addition of more walnuts.

Leaves, barks, roots, berries, flowers, vegetables and nuts make beautiful natural dyes. To extract color, let these materials simmer for at least an hour. Experiment soaking metals such as iron and copper in water to see what colors develop.

The drying time for baskets is completely dependent on the weather, much like drying laundry. The warmer the temperature, the faster the basket will dry. If outside temperatures are below freezing, it is best to dry a basket indoors. Humidity also affects the drying time, and if baskets stay damp for more than a couple of days, they may mildew.

evenly over the basket. Keeping the basket out of direct sunlight will also help the dye to dry evenly.

Chemical Dyes

Chemical dyes are laboratory-made dyes from either organic or inorganic compounds. The types most often used in basketry are direct dyes and fiber-reactive dyes.

DIRECT DYES

Direct dyes are the easiest to use, but are the least colorfast and lightfast of the three groups of dyes basketmakers generally use. Mordants of $1/4$ cup of salt in the dyebath and 1 cup of vinegar in the rinse water help to set the color.

These dyes can be saved and used again, but the colors will be

Basket dyed in a walnut hull vat. The strainer is used to skim debris off the top of the vat.

lighter as the dye is spent (the color is used up).

FIBER-REACTIVE DYES

Fiber-reactive dyes are the most colorfast and lightfast of these three groups of dyes. They are easy to mix, but it takes more skill and patience to get the color to set. The fiber-reactive dyes require a mordant for the chemical process to work, usually an alkaline solution.

These dyes cannot be saved because they lose their potency after an hour or two.

TIP

If dye bleeds onto a piece of natural weaving material, use a Q-tip and bleach to remove the stain.

When disposing of fiber-reactive dyes, do not pour them down the

Jill Choate, *Antler Egg Basket*,
dyed reed, white-tailed deer
antler, ribbed construction,
14"H x 12"Dia,
photo: M. Snively.

Jill Choate,
fanned market basket,
rattan, mule deer antler,
ribbed construction,
12"H x 22"Dia,
photo: M. Snively.

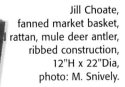

kitchen sink. Pour them in the yard away from the septic system, wells, pets and play areas. If a large amount of dye is used, a dry well is recommended to dispose of the unused portion of the dye. If a dye is used until the color is spent, it is safer to pour what's left down the drain. Spent dyes usually have too little dye left in them to cause problems to processing systems. When mordants are mixed with dyes, however, they become more caustic to humans and to plumbing. Boiling the dyes in a well-ventilated area will cause them to evaporate with very little liquid solution being left.

Storing Dyes

Only natural and direct dyes can be stored. They should be put in airtight containers such as milk jugs, away from any foodstuff, children and pets. The skull and crossbones symbol for poison should be boldly written on the container so that it is not mistaken for something to be consumed. Purple dye resembles grape punch and could easily be mistaken for a beverage. Place it away from the reach of children.

To reuse a direct dye, you may need to reheat it. Once a direct dye is stored, it will lose its depth of

Rhonda Anderson, *Sentinel*, shed antler, sweetgrass, 13"H x 7½"W x 12½"D.

Sheila King, *Points of Nature*, dyed reed, birch bark, porcupine quills, birch fungus, vines, 10"H x 12"Dia.

Left: Removing dye stain.

Below: Patti Quinn Hill, *The Wok*, rattan, lacquered ash, oak, walnut and fabric dye, 9½"H x 21"Dia.

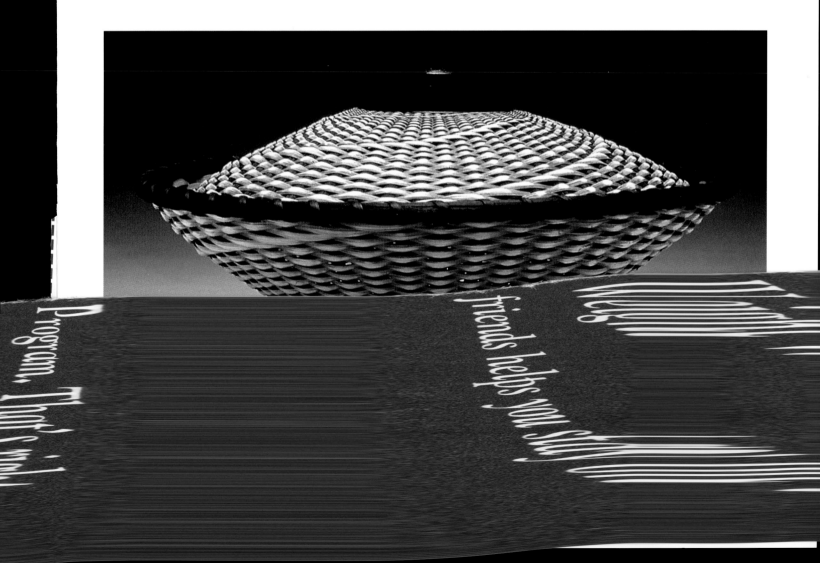

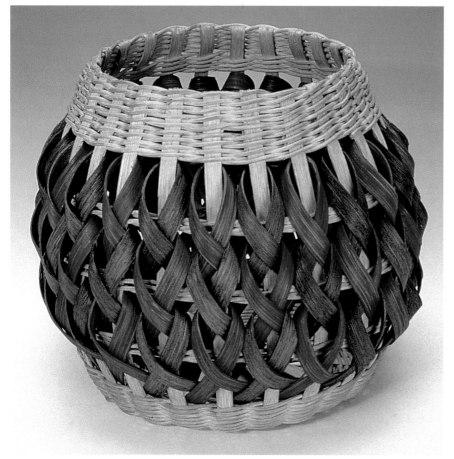

color each time it is reused. As a direct dye sits more than a day or two without being reheated, it has a tendency to become very fibrous. Because of their inexpensive cost, it is preferable not to store commercial dyes for safety reasons.

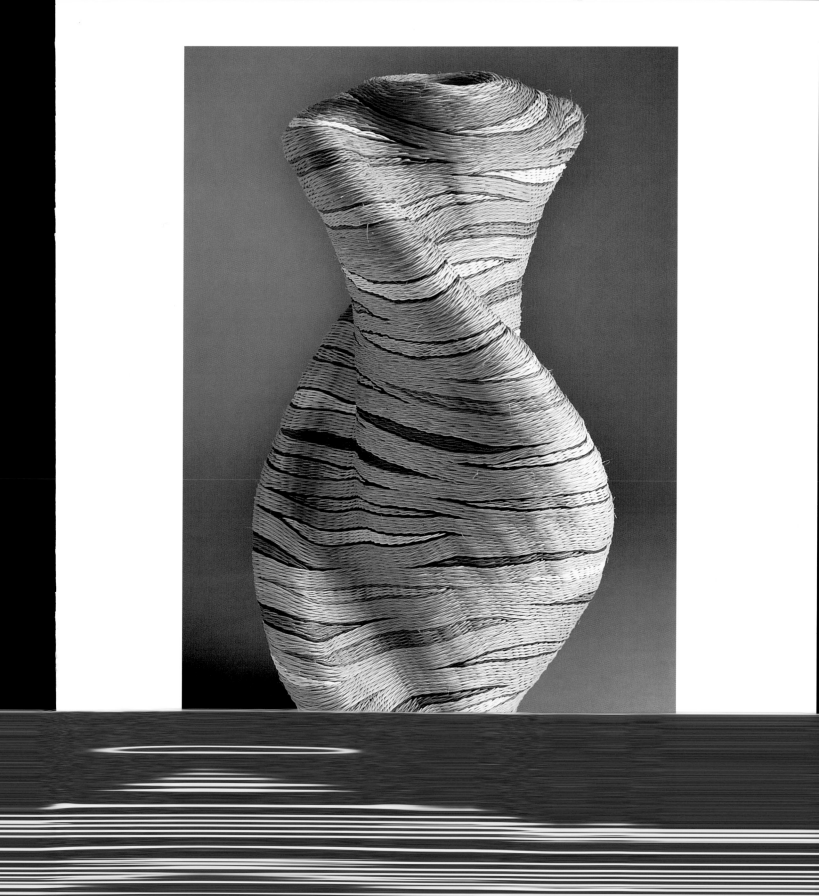

5

Stop-and-Start Plaiting

An expression frequently used in basketry is "form follows function." The Colonial Chairside Basket (instructions below) is designed to be used. The form or shape is patterned after an Appalachian market basket once used to bring the crops in from the field or to carry to market. Remember, 100 years ago there were no paper or plastic bags for storage. The swing handle adds a decorative touch and makes for easier carrying. Historically, in the South, baskets were designed with feet so air could circulate around the basket and prevent its contents from molding and mildewing.

Colonial Chairside Basket

Don't let the size discourage you. Although the basket is large, it is an easy one to make. The materials are easy to control, and the basket can be made in just a few hours' time. If you are not yet ready to experiment with dyeing reed, weave the basket using natural reed. There is beauty in simplicity.

The colors used in the basket pictured are created using direct dyes. To use a direct dye, follow the instructions on the packet and adhere to the safety precautions presented in Chapter 4.

Billie Ruth Sudduth, the *Colonial Chairside Basket*, 23"H x 13"W x 10"D.

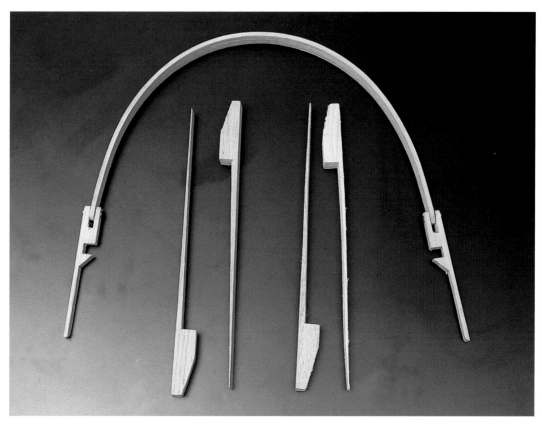

Handle and feet for the *Colonial Chairside Basket*.

Materials for the Colonial Chairside Basket

12" swing handle with brass rivets

four 10" to 12" basket feet

³⁄₄" flat reed for stakes:	cut eleven @ 38"; cut nine @ 41"
¹⁄₂" flat reed for weavers:	cut four @ 64"
³⁄₄" flat reed for weavers:	cut four @ 64"
¹⁄₄" flat reed for weavers:	cut three @ 64"
¹⁄₄" flat dyed reed for weavers:	cut eight @ 64"
⁵⁄₈" flat dyed reed for weavers:	cut two @ 64"
⁵⁄₈" flat-oval reed for rims:	cut two @ 64"
¹⁄₄" flat or ¹¹⁄₆₄" flat-oval reed for lashing:	approximately 6' (two shorter pieces may be used)
#5 round reed for rim filler:	64" length
#3 round reed for twining the base:	approximately 6' in length

Billie Ruth Sudduth, variation of the *Colonial Chairside Basket*, 12"H x 14"W x 15"D.

PREPARATION

Lightly sand the swing handle and the four basket feet. This will remove any splinters and prepare the handle and feet for later dyeing.

Determine the "good" and the "bad" side of each stake. Soak the stakes in water with the good side of the reed curved to the outside. It is easier to lay out the base with all the stakes curved in the same direction. After soaking the cut stakes in water for a few minutes, mark the midpoints on the inside of each stake. Rather than measur-

ing with a ruler or tape measure, the easiest way to find the midpoint is to gently bend the reed in half without making a crease.

WEAVING THE BASE

Lay the nine 41" stakes lengthwise, lining up the midpoint marks. Allow a half-inch space between each stake. The rough side (bad side) of the stake with the midpoint mark should be facing up. The smooth side (good side) of the stake should be flat against the

table. Check to see that the spaces between the stakes resemble squares and not rectangles.

TIP

Use a spoke weight to hold the horizontal stakes in place as they are being woven.

Weave one 38" stake across the midpoint line going over one stake, under one stake, over and under, until you have woven across all nine horizontal stakes. Weave five 38" stakes to the left of the midpoint stake and five 38" stakes to the right of the midpoint, leaving a half-inch space between each stake. When the base is woven, there should be nine horizontal stakes and 11 vertical stakes.

Base Measurements

Adjust the base to measure 13"W x 10"D. This is called "truing up" the base. It is important to be exact with the base measurements so the handle will fit. If the base is too small, the handle will hang over the ends of the completed basket. If the base is too large, the handle will fall inside the basket.

To check the depth of the basket, lay the handle on the woven base. The length may look too short, but with the measurements of 13"W x 10"D, the handle will be a perfect fit.

Twining the Base

Soak the #3 round reed and the weavers in a pan of water for a few minutes. If any weavers are dyed, soak them separately and only briefly. Twine once around the base using the #3 round reed. Begin on a long side of the base away from the corner stakes. Gently crimp the #3 round reed in half, being careful not to break it. Place the crimped end of the reed around a stake against the base of the basket. It does not matter in which direction you twine. The piece of reed that is underneath a stake will be placed on top of the next stake and the piece that was on top goes underneath. Two pieces of weaver will be moving around the base of the basket simultaneously, over and under each stake, with a half-twist between each stake.

This is a locking weave and will hold all the base stakes in place. If the twining pulls under a corner, reverse the position of the twining so it will lock at the corner. When the starting point is reached, whip the loose ends under previous rows

Billie Ruth Sudduth, collection of nested, plaited baskets (based on Sosse Baker's checkerboard design).

of twining and cut the excess.

Upsett the basket (see Chapter 3). Once all stakes are bent over flat against the base, lay a spoke weight on the base to help it sit flat.

WEAVING THE SIDES

The first two rows of any basket are always the most difficult. Don't let this discourage you. Even experienced weavers make mistakes at this point. As you are weaving the sides, remember: *over and under*.

The shape of the basket is crucial for the accurate fit of the handle. As the sides are being woven, visualize the same amount of space between the stakes continuing up the basket.

Mistakes occur most often at the corners. Make sure that the over-one-stake, under-one-stake pattern continues and that you keep the tension even as the corners are rounded. This will prevent the corners from becoming too tight or too loose. It is helpful to

TECHNIQUES FOR WEAVING THE COLONIAL CHAIRSIDE BASKET

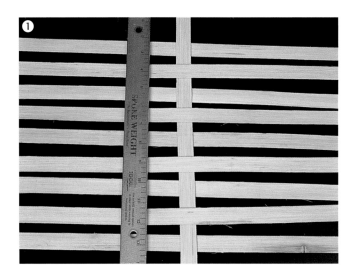

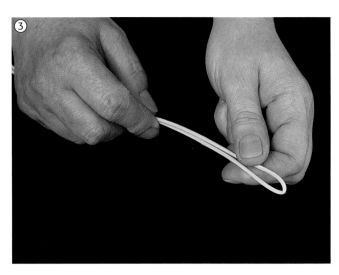

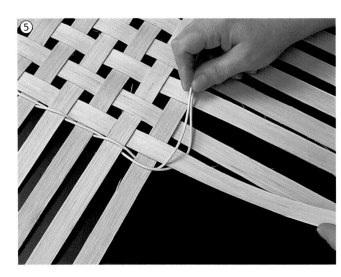

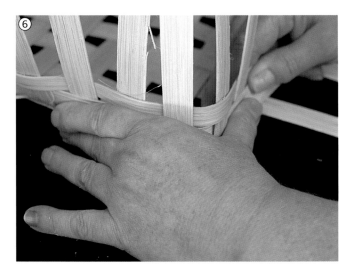

1 A spoke weight holds the horizontal stakes in place as they are woven.

2 Using the handle to check the depth of the basket.

3 Crimping the twining.

4 Twining the base.

5 Twining around a corner.

6 Controlling the tension of the weaver as the corner is rounded.

7 Beginning the first row of weaving on the inside of a stake.

8 Inserting the handle on the inside of the basket.

9 Attaching the rim.

10 Inserting the feet along a stake.

Rowena Bradley, rivercane Cherokee basket, plaited and twill woven, 11"H x 14"W x 15"D.

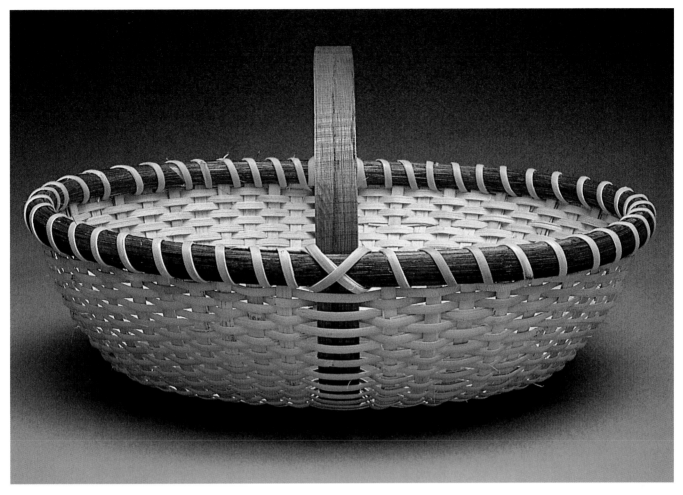

Patti Simmons, *False Impressions*, oak, cane, wood base, red mahogany stain, plaited, 8"H x 12"W x 9½"D.

cup the corners in your hand as you round them to help control the tension.

The plaited sides are woven in the stop/start method of weaving. To begin, place the end of a ¹/₂" flat weaver on the inside of the basket behind a stake. The smooth side of the weaver should be facing the outside of the basket. Secure in place with a clothespin. Moving counterclockwise around the basket (clockwise if you are left-handed), weave over one stake, under one stake, over and under, until the starting point is reached. Pass the starting point by two stakes and cut the end of the weaver. Place the loose ends of the weaver behind a stake so they will not be visible from the inside or the outside of the basket. If the loose ends are still showing, reverse their placement, as explained in Chapter 3.

Pattern for the Sides

The following pattern is used for the sides of the *Colonial Chairside Basket*:

Row 1	¹/₂" flat
Row 2	³/₄" flat
Row 3	¹/₄" flat (dyed)
Row 4	¹/₄" flat (dyed)
Row 5	⁵/₈" flat (dyed)
Row 6	¹/₄" flat (dyed)
Row 7	¹/₄" flat (dyed)
Row 8	¹/₂" flat
Row 9	³/₄" flat
Row 10	¹/₄" flat
Row 11	¹/₄" flat
Row 12	¹/₄" flat
Row 13	³/₄" flat
Row 14	¹/₂" flat
Row 15	¹/₄" flat (dyed)
Row 16	¹/₄" flat (dyed)
Row 17	⁵/₈" flat (dyed)
Row 18	¹/₄" flat (dyed)
Row 19	¹/₄" flat (dyed)
Row 20	³/₄" flat
Row 21	¹/₂" flat
Rim Row	⁵/₈" flat-oval

Begin the second row of weaving on the opposite side of the basket from the first row. Place the end of the weaver behind a stake that has a piece of weaver woven in front of it on row one. Proceed around the basket with row two. The overs and unders of this row should be opposite those of the first row. This is the meaning of weaving: *over and under*. Alternate beginning and ending each row on opposite sides of the basket to prevent a stacked appearance or obvious bulge.

The tension of the weaving and the spaces between the stakes should remain constant as the sides are being woven. This will prevent the top from flaring out or pulling in too tightly. After every few rows of weaving, pack each row tightly against the row below it to eliminate unwanted spaces in the sides of the basket.

Bend and Tuck

After the top row is woven, bend and tuck following the directions in Chapter 3.

INSERTING A HANDLE

The handle is inserted on the inside of the basket along the middle 38" vertical stake on each side of the basket. When the handle is in place, there should be five stakes to the right of the handle and five stakes to the left. Because of the thickness of the handle, skip several rows of weaving before beginning to insert. The rim will secure the handle at the notches.

Follow the directions for carving a rim in Chapter 3. Place a piece of $5/8$" flat-oval reed around the inside and outside top row of weaving, overlapping away from the handle. Insert a piece of #5 round reed between the rim pieces, butting the ends slightly off-center

at the handle. Lash the rims together with $1/4$" flat reed or $11/64$" flat-oval reed. Weave an "X" at the handle with the lashing to secure it in place. The lashing will cross behind the handle diagonally on the inside of the basket, come to the outside crossing the handle and pass to the inside again. The lashing will again come to the outside and cross diagonally to form the X. There will not be an X formed on the inside of the basket.

INSERTING FEET

Insert the feet along each corner stake on the long side of the basket. They will be inserted under the rows of weaving on the outside of the basket along a stake. The feet

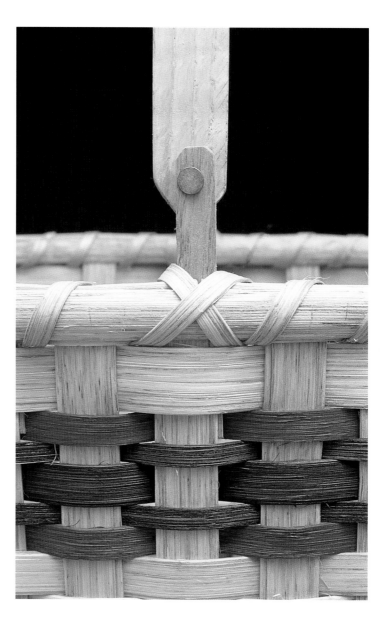

Weaving an "X" at the handle to secure it.

Left: David Paul Bacharach, *Wye River Morning*, copper, bronze, chemical patina, woven, constructed, 20"H x 10½"Dia.

Below: Joyce Schaum, bushel basket, dyed reed, oak handles, plaited, 21½"H x 15"Dia.

Billie Ruth Sudduth, plaited elbow basket, 25"H x 21"W x 6½"D.

Nadine Tuttle, plaited willow tree inner bark, rim bark wearing its outer bark, Emu feather, 5"H x 10"W x 5"D.

are held in place by the weaving. If they are too long, cut off the excess before inserting.

A plain filler is used for the base.

Upon completion, the basket should measure 23"H (including the handle) x 13"W x 10"D. Dyeing it in a vat of walnut-hull dye will give the basket an aged appearance. Follow the recommendations for dyeing and drying in Chapter 4.

VARIATIONS

To change the appearance of the *Colonial Chairside Basket*, bushel handles can be used rather than a swing handle. The feet can also be eliminated.

Plaited baskets are among the easiest to weave in a variety of sizes with varying widths of materials. To make larger plaited baskets, use a larger width of reed for the stakes. Any size reed can be used for the weavers. A smaller size stake is used for smaller plaited baskets. Smaller size weaving materials require more rows of weaving.

Use the *Colonial Chairside Basket* as a guide to design a plaited basket that is uniquely your own. First determine the size of the basket you want to make. The length of the stakes is calculated by adding the dimensions of the height twice to the width once, plus four to six inches for bending and tucking. These will be the measurements for the vertical stakes. To determine the length of the horizontal stakes, add the height twice to the length once, plus four to six inches for bending and tucking. This formula will apply to almost any basket. The length of the weaver is determined by adding the width twice to the depth twice, plus four to six inches for overlapping.

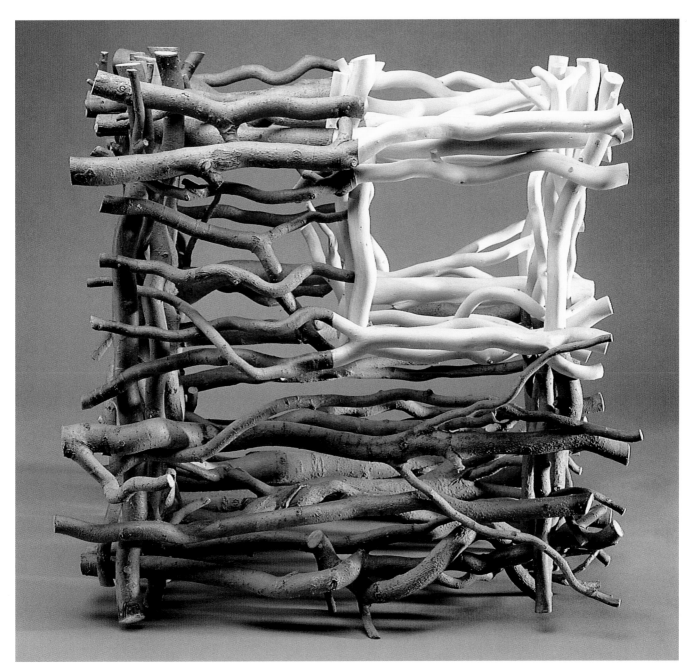

Dorothy Gill Barnes, *Willow with White Window*, corkscrew willow partly peeled, peg construction, 24"H x 24"W x 22"D, photo: Doug Martin.

6

Continuous Plaiting

In the late 1700s and early 1800s, the Shakers became well known for their basketmaking as they established a commercial endeavor to produce income for the sect. They used molds extensively for uniformity of shape as well as simplicity of design. Many of the molds were used to create cat-head-shaped baskets which sat on four feet. If the basket were turned upside down, the feet of the basket resembled the ears of a cat. The cat's head became the body of the basket.

Shaker Cat's Head Wall Basket

This basket is inspired by the baskets of the Shakers, with one major difference: there is no mold. The basket is shaped entirely by hand so no two will be exactly alike. The *Shaker Cat's Head Wall Basket* is designed to hang on the wall. However, because of the shape, the basket looks stunning perched on its feet.

Fred Ely, *Rain*, cherry, cane, dyed porcupine quills, photo: Don Rutt.

Billie Ruth Sudduth, *Shaker Cat's Head Wall Basket*, dyed reed, oak, plaited, 10"H x 8½"W x 3½"D.

Materials for the Shaker Cat's Head Wall Basket

7 mm flat-oval European cut reed for stakes	cut seven @ 35"
	cut 17 @ 31"
¹¹⁄₆₄" flat-oval European cut reed for weavers	three to four long natural pieces
	12 to 15 long dyed pieces
7 mm flat for rim row	cut one @ 30"
³⁄₈" flat-oval for rim	cut two pieces @ 30"
3" notched-side oak handle	
¹¹⁄₆₄" flat-oval European cut reed for lashing	one long natural piece

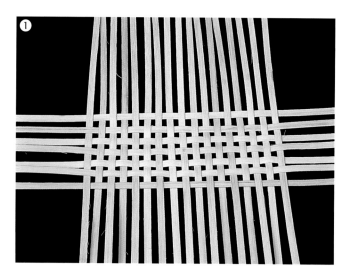

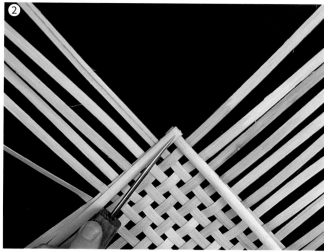

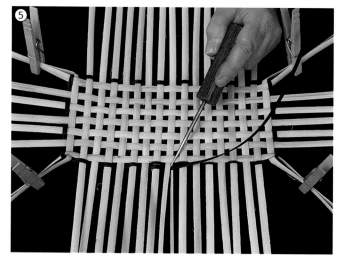

1 *Shaker Cat's Head Wall Basket* base.
2 Upsetting the four corners.
3 Splitting a stake.
4 Tapered weaver behind the stake to the left of the split stake.
5 Beginning row 2.

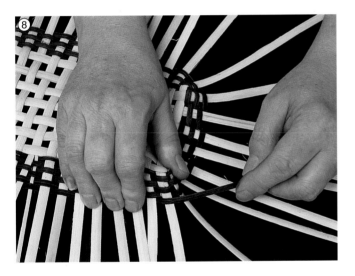

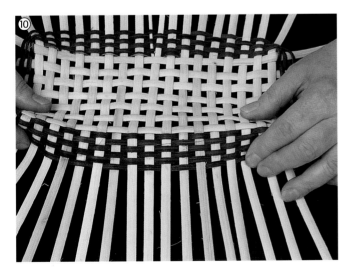

6 Using the handle as a guide for the placement of the base stakes.
7 Flared base at row 5.
8 Increasing tension at the corners.
9 Bending base against a flat table edge.
10 Shaping the corners.

11 Changing weaving from dark to natural.
12 Tapered weaver at the end of the last row of weaving.
13 Inserting the handle.

PREPARATION

Lightly sand the handle. Soak the materials briefly in a pan of water to make them more pliable. If dyed reed is used, soak it separately and only briefly to keep the colors from bleeding on the other weaving materials. This basket is beautiful when woven with two colors. Refer to Chapter 4 for information on dyes and dyeing. Follow the manufacturer's directions when using commercial dyes and always adhere to safety guidelines. The *Cat's Head Basket* is also distinctive—and more closely resembles the original Shaker baskets—when it's left natural.

WEAVING THE BASE

The stakes are laid out in the same manner as the *Colonial Chairside Basket* in Chapter 5. The flat side of the stakes will be facing up and the flat-oval side will be lying against the table. The base is laid out with the inside of the basket facing up. There are seven horizontal stakes and 17 vertical stakes. When all stakes are in place, the base should measure $8^1/_2$"W x $3^1/_2$"D. True up or adjust the base of the basket to these measurements. Do not upsett the basket. Only the pairs of stakes at each of the four corners will be upsett. This is done to create the basket feet.

Splitting a Stake

In order to follow a continuous weaving pattern, a stake is split, which results in an odd number of stakes. Otherwise, a stake would have to be added or a step-up twill would have to be woven on every row to proceed continuously. Carefully split the middle stake on one of the long sides of the basket. This

Jackie Abrams, *Urn of Violets*, paper, paint, waxed linen, varnish, 9"H x 11"W x 11"D, photo: Greg Hubbard.

Johanna Heller, *Garlic Pot*, fretwork base, reed, seagrass, plaited, 6"H x 8"Dia.

Takesonosai, untitled basket, smoked bamboo, photo: Textile Arts Gallery, Santa Fe, New Mexico.

will become the back of the basket. Split or cut the stake all the way to the plaited base, being careful not to cut the stake off. The split stake should be as even as you can cut it. There will now be two separate stakes where there was originally one.

WEAVING THE SIDES

When weaving continuously, an adjustment can be made to the weaver so the beginning of the weaving won't be noticeable. Using sharp scissors or cutters, taper one end of a weaver for several inches, proceeding from a very narrow taper to the original width of the weaver. This is the only tapering necessary until the last five rows of weaving at the top of the basket.

After the stake is split and the

Alice Ogden, low fruit basket, black ash, white oak, mold woven, 12"H x 8"Dia and 4"H x 3"Dia, photo: Charley Fryebury.

first weaver tapered, turn the basket base over. The flat-oval side of the stakes will be facing up with the flat side against the table. Clothespin the two stakes at each corner together. Insert the tapered weaver behind the stake to the left of the split stake on the back of the basket. The flat-oval side of the weaver will be facing the outside of the basket. Begin the weaving pattern of over one stake, under one stake, around the basket base one full revolution. On this first round, treat the split stake as if it had not been cut. When the split stake is reached on the second round, the weaving pattern of over one, under one will continue automatically.

Now the split stake is treated as two separate stakes. The first row of weaving will be the locking row, so twining the base is not necessary. Adjust the base stakes for the handle to fit along the second stake on either side of the split stake. These stakes may need to be moved slightly to the right or left for the handle to line up with the stakes.

TIP

Use the handle as a guide for the placement of the base stakes. It is easier to adjust the measurements at the beginning than after the basket has been woven.

The weave of over one, under one on the second row will be opposite the overs and unders of the first row. When the original weaver runs out, add a new piece as described in Chapter 3. The original and the new weaver will overlap for two stakes. None of the added weavers should be tapered. Check to see that the loose ends are not visible from the inside or the outside of the basket.

Shaping

Keep the two stakes at each corner clothespinned together while weaving the first five rows. This will help in creating the cat's-head shape. As the weaving progresses,

Anonymous, Vietnamese winnowing basket, bamboo, plaited, 16"Dia.

fan the stakes out and widen the flare of the base. This must be done on each row and at every corner for the basket to have the desired shape. The basket is actually being woven upside down for the first several rows.

After row five is complete, remove the clothespins but continue fanning out the base. Continue weaving in this manner until the spaces between each stake are fairly consistent. As the first five rows are being woven, increase the tension on the weaver when going around the corners. Initially the corners will be pinched together to make the base "kick up." As the weaving proceeds up the basket, begin to cup the corners in your hand as you round them. Pull the corners in toward the base of the basket.

When 12 to 15 rows have been completed, bend each side of the base against a flat table edge. This is similar to upsetting, but is done much later in the weaving process to obtain the cat's-head shape. Place the basket back on the table and continue weaving upside down for several more rows. You will continue to increase the tension on the corners as you pull them in against the base. The stakes will also continue to flare out. Between rows 15 and 20, a very pronounced kicked-up shape should appear.

Flip the position of the basket at row 20 and begin weaving right side up. This is where the success of your shaping will become obvious. The basket should already be sitting on its feet and the stakes should flare out. The weaving for the remainder of the basket will concentrate on bringing the stakes in toward each other so the opening at the top is at least as small as the area of the base. Continue until 52 rows have been woven.

Marion and Arthur
Landfors, *Nantucket Purse*,
cherry, oak, ivory,
8"H x 8½"W x 6½"D.

For the sides of the basket to curve in, increase the tension on the weaving, taking care not to pull too tightly.

Changing Color

If the basket is woven with two colors, change from dyed to natural weavers at row 53. Lay the end of the dyed reed on top of the end of the natural reed in the area of the split stake and continue weaving for five more rows. When the basket is completed, the color change will be obscure. Taper the end of the weaver and end at the split stake.

Bending and Tucking

At this stage of the basket, there should be 52 rows woven with dyed reed and five rows woven with natural reed for a total of 57 rows of weaving. If no color is used, all 57 rows will be natural. Weave a rim row using 7 mm flat reed. Bend the outside stakes to the inside of the basket and tuck them under the third row of weaving. Cut the inside stakes even with the top row of weaving.

INSERTING THE HANDLE

The handle will be inserted along the stakes on the back side of the basket where the stake is split. It will be inserted below the five natural rows of weaving and along the third stake on either side of the split stake. The stakes can still be manipulated to accommodate the handle.

Carving and Attaching a Rim

The outside rim piece will overlap on the back side of the basket between the stakes where the handle is inserted. The inside rim will overlap behind the rim row on the front side of the basket. To prevent the rims from appearing bulky, overlap the inside and outside rim in different places.

Billie Ruth Sudduth, *Shaker Cat's Head Wall Basket*, dyed reed, oak, 10"H x 8½"W x 3½"D.

Lash the rims together following the instructions for lashing in Chapter 3. Begin and end the lashing on one end of the basket. It will be less noticeable there.

It is almost never too late to correct some problems with a basket. If the weaving is not tight enough, it can be pulled tighter with an awl and worked into the basket. This is called "getting the air out."

TIP

If your basket does not sit level, manipulate the feet from the outside of the basket or push the feet out from the inside of the basket.

Use a cotton swab with bleach to remove any dye that bled onto other weaving materials. When the basket is cleaned up and any fuzz or hairs removed, it can be overdyed in a vat of walnut-hull dye. Turn it from side to side so it will dry evenly.

COLOR VARIATIONS

To change the appearance of the basket, experiment with different color combinations. The stakes, the top five rows, and the rim should all be the same color, with the weavers a different color. Even the handle can be dyed.

David Paul Bacharach, *Enfield*, chimney vessel, woven copper/bronze rim, patinated with heat and chemicals, 17"H x 9"W x 8"D.

Twined Construction

Marilyn Moore, *Sentinels*, copper and magnet wire, stainless steel mesh, twined, 8½"H x 6"Dia, photo: William Wickett.

The basket described in this chapter was designed and named in honor of a very special place in North Carolina: Penland School. When I first made it, I used very vivid turquoise and peach colors for the frame and the braids. From a distance, the braids appeared as if they were made from clay. When black dyes are used for the braids, they appear as leather. Perhaps other dyes could be tried and a series developed as a tribute to other craft mediums.

Twining means weaving two weavers simultaneously, one going in front of a spoke and the other behind the same spoke, with a half twist in between. *Wales* are a variation of twining using more than two weavers. When three weavers are used together, it is called three-rod wale; four weavers, four-rod wale; and so on. Twining is an easy technique to learn and one that moves rather quickly.

Twining almost always uses round reed or some other round material for the weaving, but the stakes or spokes can be flat or round. The technique is the same for both, with the exception of adding a weaver. When twining around round spokes, weave with the end of the old weaver and the beginning of the new weaver together for three or four spokes to

Karyl Sisson, *Vessel XXI*, cotton twill tape, dyed miniature clothespins, twined and stitched, 7"H x 16"W x 14"D, photo: Susan Einstein.

Diana Macomber, *Pair Standing Canada Geese*, vine rattan, single-strand wire, randing, twining, 17"H x 19"W x 11"D, 20"H x 18"W x 10"D, photo: Steven C. Tuttle.

TWINING A ROUND-SPOKE BASE

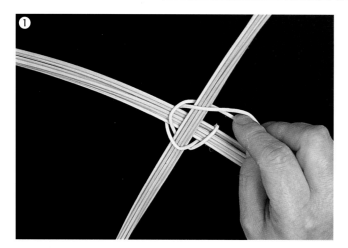

1 Twining the first row around groups of round spokes.

2 Twining and spacing subsequent rows. In this example, spaces are left between the rows.

secure the loose ends. Spaces can be left between the twined rows, or the rows can be packed tightly against each other.

Because twining materials are very flexible and pliable, a wide variety of shapes are possible. These materials can easily be mixed with other materials and techniques. Twining is also useful as a method to secure the base of a basket before it is upsett, or it can be used to construct the entire frame, as in the *Penland Pottery Basket*.

Penland Pottery Basket

PREPARATION

Cut 72 pieces of $^1/_2$" flat reed and dye them a dark color. (Refer to Chapter 4 for dyeing information.) Soak the spokes and round reed in water for a few minutes.

TIP

Round reed breaks more easily than flat reed, so it will require a longer soaking time.

Mark the midpoints on all 12 spokes on the rough side. Mark 2" on each side of the center on six of these spokes.

WEAVING THE BASE

Twining is the only weaving technique used to construct the frame of the *Penland Pottery Basket.*

Fan the six spokes which are marked 2" from the center into a circle, lining up the midpoint marks and spacing evenly between each. Lay a spoke weight across the middle to hold the spokes in place while twining once around the base, beginning at the 2" marks. Remove the spoke weight and twine a total of six rows.

Polly Adams Sutton, *Horsetail Root*, cedar bark, horsetail root, twined, 4"H x 7"Dia, photo: Bill Wickett.

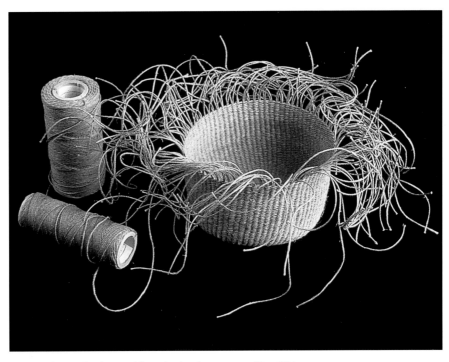

Tressa Sularz, twined waxed linen basket in process, 4"H x 7"Dia.

Billie Ruth Sudduth, *Penland Pottery Basket*, dyed reed, twined and braided, 8"H x 10"W x 10"D.

When the weaver runs out, tuck the end under the twining along a spoke. Insert the end of a new weaver into the same space and continue twining. Add the remaining six spokes one at a time, twining in place between the existing spokes. Continue twining until the base measures 8" across.

An alternate method of laying out the base is to stack the six spokes with the mark 2" from the center on top of each other, lining up the midpoint marks. Secure the spokes on a board with a t-pin and then fan them out. Twine around the spokes six rounds, then remove the base from the board and proceed as above.

Until this stage, the weaving has been on the inside of the basket, rough side up, with the base flat against the table. Now, pick up the basket and continue twining on the outside of the basket for six to eight more rows, pulling gently on the twining to round the spokes upward from the base. The spokes are not upsett or creased, but are gently rounded upward as a result of the tension placed on the weavers. When these rows are completed, the ends of the twining will lay

Materials for Penland Pottery Basket

³⁄₈" flat reed for spokes	cut 12 @ 32"
#3 round reed for twining	10-12 pieces at least 60"
¹⁄₂" flat reed for braids	cut 72 @ 9"

MAKING THE PENLAND POTTERY BASKET

1 Materials for the *Penland Pottery Basket*.

2 Marking the midpoints.

3 Laying out the base spokes.
4 Beginning twining around the base spokes.
5 Adding a weaver.
6 Inserting the second set of spokes.
7 Measuring at 8" for the base.
8 Twining up the basket.

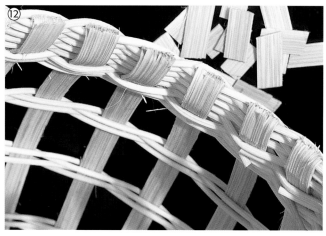

against a spoke on the inside of the basket.

WEAVING THE SIDES

On every other spoke, mark 1½" up the spoke from the point where the twining ends; mark 1½" up from this point again, then repeat two more times. The spokes will have four marks on them at 1½" intervals.

Twine around each 1½" mark for two rows, starting slightly be-low the mark so the second round of twining will be at the mark. The twining should be long enough to go around the perimeter of the basket two times without having to add a new weaver.

The first two rows of twining should be the same tension as the base. The second set should be looser. When twining around the third 1½" mark, gently increase the tension on the twining to make the basket curve in. At the fourth 1½" mark, twine for eight rows,

9 Marking spokes at 1½" intervals.
10 Shape of the *Penland Pottery Basket* when the twining is complete.
11 Bending spokes to the inside of the basket and tucking.
12 Spokes tucked under twining on the inside of the basket.
13 "Kicking in" the base.

pulling each row tighter than the preceding row.

BENDING AND TUCKING

Soak the spokes above the twining. Bend each spoke to the inside of the basket and cut the excess reed that goes below the twining. The spoke will lay over three or four rows of twining and tuck under the remaining rows. "Kick" in the base of the basket by pressing against it. This will make the basket sit flat. If the basket frame is to be dyed, it should be done next, before the braids are inserted.

BRAIDING THE SIDES

Braiding is the method I used to weave color into the *Penland Pottery Basket* and was designed specifically for this basket. It is done by inserting short pieces of weaving along individual spokes in sets of

Sue Kolvereid, *Genie of the Deer Yard*, knothole honeysuckle, outer white cedar bark, deer toe bones, grouse feathers, twined, 9"H x 6"Dia, photo: Bruce Blank.

MAKING THE PENLAND POTTERY BASKET

14 Inserting the first braid.

15 Crisscrossing the first twining line.

16 Inserting the second braid.

Marilyn Sharp, *Round and Round*, paper rush, waxed thread, ti twining, 11"H x 10"W x 10"D, photo: R.C. Sharp.

Repeat twice more down the spoke. Use another $1/2$" piece, taking it behind the spoke below the top row of twining and bringing it to the outside of the spoke. As these pieces are crisscrossed to lay behind the third row of twining, they will be caught under the ends of the first braid. The third braid begins under the second row of twining, comes to the outside, crisscrosses, catches the second braid to the inside, and lays against the base of the basket.

The ends of all the braids will show on the inside of the basket, adding an interesting texture to the finished piece.

Suggested color variations are pictured in Chapter 4. Try various color combinations to see how color affects the character of the basket. Since the basket uses a lot of $1/2$" scraps, it is an excellent basket to experiment with color.

Ti-Twined Baskets

Most twined baskets, such as the *Penland Pottery Basket*, use flexible materials. *Ti-twined* or *wrapped-twined* baskets differ from these in that rigid spokes are used. Of the two weavers, one is rigid and one is flexible. The rigid weaver is placed on the inside of the spoke; then, where it crosses the spoke, it's bound or wrapped in place by the flexible weaver. The designs are introduced by moving the inside weaver to the outside. This is an ancient technique used by the Poma, Yurok and Makah of the western United States. The materials they used included willow, roots and grasses.

Once you have mastered working with flexible materials, you may want to try a ti-twined basket.

three, working from the top of the spoke to the base. Once the rim is complete, three double rows of twining will show between the base and the rim, spaced approximately $1^1/2$" apart. The braids will be inserted from the top row down on each spoke, one spoke at a time.

Check the length of the braids before beginning. The braids should only be long enough to lay on the inside of the basket without popping out. The tighter the weave, the shorter the braids will need to be.

Place a 9" piece of the dyed $1/2$" reed behind a spoke, rough side to rough side. This piece will go directly under the rim, above the first double row of twining. Bring the ends of this $1/2$" piece to the front on each side of the existing spoke. Crisscross over the twining line and have each end lay behind the second double row of twining on the inside of the basket.

Ann Hall-Richards, *Emerging from the Layers*, cast paper, waxed linen, twined, 19½"H x 7"W x 2½"D, photo: Warwick Green Photography.

Stop-and-Start Twill Weave

he double-bottom Calabash Clam Basket is affectionately named for the little seaside village of Calabash, which is on the extreme southeastern coast of North Carolina and is famous for its shrimp boats. The name has a double meaning: the basket is strong enough to hold clams, and the pattern is named for the bivalve clam. This "Chevron" pattern is a signature of the Chitimachas along the Gulf Coast of Louisiana, but their arrow design is usually not woven over the entire basket.

The distinguishing characteristics of twill weaves are weaving over and under more than one element at a time and the diagonal pattern the weave creates. In a twill woven basket, each new row is started by stepping over one stake or spoke from the last row. This construction results in some of the most interesting designs in basketry where pattern, sequence and proportion are evident.

The base of the basket can be a twill weave, or the sides can be a twill, or else the entire basket can be a twill. The twill can also be interchanged with plaiting to add to the visual excitement of the design.

Billie Ruth Sudduth, *Calabash Clam Basket*, dyed reed, oak, twill weave, 18"H x 14"Dia.

Graph paper can be used to design various twill designs.

Twill weave can be stop-and-start (one row at a time) or continuous, balanced or unbalanced. A twill is balanced if the number of elements woven over and under are the same, for example, going over two spokes and under two spokes. A twill is unbalanced if the number of elements woven over varies from the number of elements woven under. An example of an unbalanced twill is weaving over three spokes and under two spokes. When a twill is balanced, it is easier to control the tension of the weave, and it usually creates a stronger basket. Experiment with the endless possibilities of the overs and unders and the patterns created.

Calabash Clam Basket

PREPARATION

If dyed reed is used for the weavers, it should be dyed before beginning construction of the basket. Refer to Chapter 4 on dyes and dyeing.

Taper the ends of the handle to approximately ³/₈" width. This width will allow the handle to be inserted along the inside of the basket without being visible on the outside. It may help to soak the ends before tapering. Do not soak the entire handle or it will lose its steam-bent shape.

The base of this basket is similar to the *Penland Pottery* base in Chapter 7, although more spokes are used. Cut and soak the twenty ³/₄" spokes cut 40" long. Soak with the good side curved to the outside.

Soak the #3 round reed. Mark the midpoint on all the spokes on

Materials for the Calabash Clam Basket	
³/₄" flat reed for spokes	cut 20 @ 40"
#3 round reed for base twining	8-10 long pieces
7 mm flat-oval dyed for the weavers	cut and dye 31 @ 50"
³/₈" flat reed for the rim row	cut 1 @ 50"
¹/₂" flat-oval for the rim	cut 2 @ 50"
#5 round reed for the rim filler	cut 1 @ 50"
¹¹/₆₄" flat-oval lashing	1-2 long pieces
14" square notched handle with hand hold	

TECHNIQUES FOR WEAVING THE CALABASH CLAM BASKET

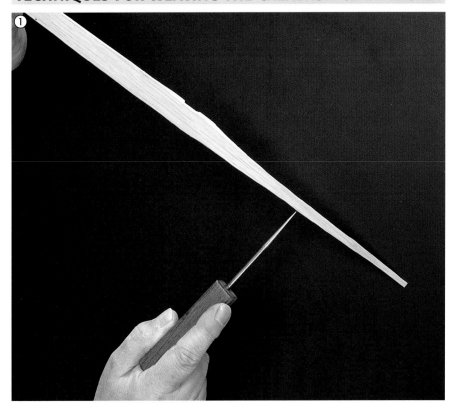

1 Tapering a handle.

the rough side. Mark 3¹/₄" on each side of the midpoint on ten of the spokes. Stack the ten marked spokes on top of each other, lining up the midpoint marks. The rough side of the spokes should be facing up. Fan the spokes out, spacing evenly between each. Use a spoke weight to hold the spokes in place. The 3¹/₄" marks on each side of the center should be lined up in a circle.

Beginning at the 3¹/₄" mark, twine with #3 round reed, packing each row against the previous row. Twine for three inches. Add the remaining ten spokes, one at a time, twining in place between each existing spoke. Continue twining until the base measures 14" in diameter. Stop the twining on the same spoke you began, hiding the ends of the #3 round reed along a base spoke. Adjust the base to fit the 14" handle.

SPLITTING SPOKES

With sharp scissors or cutters, very carefully split (cut) the base spokes lengthwise from the end of the spoke to the last row of twining. Upsett the basket by bending the spokes to the inside of the basket along the last row of twining.

WEAVING THE SIDES

The chevron pattern on the sides of the basket is created by using a step-up twill. The sides are woven in a stair-step technique using the stop-and-start method of weaving. It does not matter in which direction the step-up twill begins to create the design. However, if a set of baskets are being made, the weave for each should begin in the same direction. The baskets shown use a step-up twill first to the left and then to the right.

For the first row of weaving, treat each cut spoke as one single spoke. Weave over two spokes and under two spokes around the basket.

> **TIP**
>
> **Use a lot of clothespins on the first few rows to hold the weaving in place.**

The flat-oval side of the weaver will be facing the outside of the basket. After row one is complete, stair-step or step up each starting row one spoke to the left, treating each split spoke separately. Weave 16 rows, stair-stepping the beginning of each new row one spoke to the left.

Jimmie Kent, Calabash variation, oak, dyed reed, twill and reverse twill, 20"H x 14"Dia.

TECHNIQUES FOR WEAVING THE CALABASH CLAM BASKET

2 Adjusting the base to fit width of the handle.

3 Splitting the spokes.

4 Upsetting the basket.
5 Row one of the twill weave.
6 Changing the direction of the twill pattern.
7 Bending and tucking the spokes.
8 "Kicking" in the base.
9 Handle inserted inside the basket and lashed at the notch.

John Skau, *Blue and Red Flame*, *Ballooned Basket* series, maple, wood dye, varnish, tubular plaiting, 3/2 twill, 38"H x 18"Dia.

Claudia Leo, Chitimacha tray variation, dyed rattan, twill weave, 20" square.

REVERSING THE TWILL

To reverse or zigzag the design, row 17 will begin by stepping one spoke to the right (the opposite direction from which you have been stepping).

Continue weaving each remaining row by stepping one spoke to the right at the beginning of each new row. Continually check the spokes to keep them perpendicular to the base with equal spacing between each. Complete 15 rows, stepping to the right. Keep the tension on the weaver the same for these remaining 15 rows.

When 31 rows are woven, 16 rows of the pattern will step to the left and 15 rows will step to the right. The last row will be the rim row and will be woven with $3/8$" flat. When weaving the rim row, treat each split pair as a single spoke.

RIM AND HANDLE

Soak and bend the pairs of outside spokes to the inside of the basket and tuck under the first available row of weaving, trimming the excess. Cut the inside pair of spokes flush with the top row of weaving. Turn the basket upside down and "kick" in the bottom so the basket will sit flat.

Insert the handle along a cut spoke on the inside of the basket— it does not matter which one, as long as the handle is inserted into the same spoke on each side of the basket and is centered. The tapered ends of the handle will be secured under several rows of weaving along a split spoke toward the base. The portion of the handle near the notch is too wide to slide under the weaving, but will be secured by the rim. The handle will be lashed into place at the notch.

Place a piece of $1/2$" flat-oval reed along the inside and outside top row of weaving, flat-oval side facing out, securing the handle at the notch. Lay a piece of #5 round reed between the rims, butting the ends on the outside of the handle, slightly off center. Treat the split spokes as separate spokes and lash between each with $11/64$" flat-oval, forming an X at the handle.

Billie Ruth Sudduth, set of *Calabash Clam Baskets*, dyed reed, oak, twill weave, 6" to 14"Dia.

Materials and Instructions for Smaller Calabash Clam Baskets

6" Calabash Clam Basket

6" Diameter • 9" High

12 – $^3/_8$" spokes @ 20"

Mark 1$^1/_2$" from center on 6

• Twine with #2 round for 1"

Add remaining spokes

• Twine until base measures 6"

Weave with $^{11}/_{64}$" dyed flat-oval (25 @ 23")

• 13 left / 12 right

Rim row $^1/_4$" flat

Rim $^3/_8$" flat-oval

#4 round rim filler

$^{11}/_{64}$" flat-oval lasher

6" square notched handle with hand hold

8" Calabash Clam Basket

8" Diameter • 11" High

14 – $^1/_2$" spokes @ 25"

Mark 2" from center on 7

• Twine with #3 round for 1"

Add remaining spokes

• Twine until base measures 8"

Weave with $^{11}/_{64}$" dyed flat-oval (31 @ 30")

• 16 left / 15 right

Rim row $^3/_8$" flat

Rim $^1/_2$" flat-oval

#5 round rim filler

$^{11}/_{64}$" flat-oval lasher

8" square notched handle with hand hold

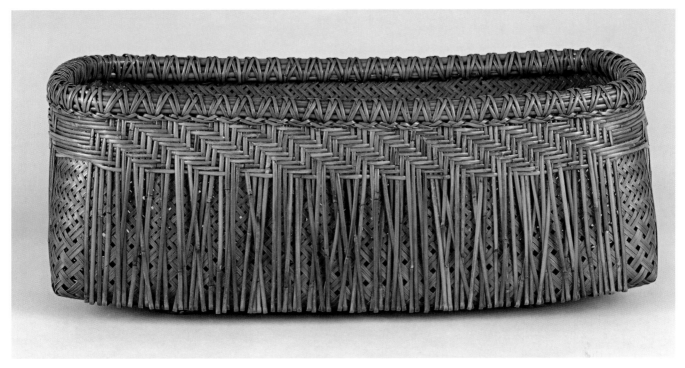

Soho Katsushiro, *Wheat Harvest*, dyed bamboo, twill weave, $8^1/_2$"H x 17"W x 8"D, photo: Textile Arts Gallery, Santa Fe, NM.

Materials and Instructions for Smaller Calabash Clam Baskets

10" Calabash Clam Basket

10" Diameter   13" High

16 – $^5/_8$" spokes @ 30"

Mark 2" from center on 8

• Twine with #3 round for 2"

Add remaining spokes

• Twine until base measures 10"

Weave with $^3/_{16}$" flat-oval (31 @ 38") dyed

• 16 left / 15 right

Rim row $^3/_8$" flat

Rim $^1/_2$" flat-oval

#5 round rim filler

$^{11}/_{64}$" flat-oval lasher

10" square notched handle with hand hold

12" Calabash Clam Basket

12" Diameter   15" High

18 – $^3/_4$" spokes @ 36"

Mark 3" from center on 9

• Twine with #3 round for $2^1/_2$"

Add remaining spokes

• Twine until base measures 12"

Weave with 7 mm dyed flat-oval (27 @ 45")

• 14 left / 13 right

Rim row $^3/_8$" flat

Rim $^1/_2$" flat-oval

#5 round rim filler

$^{11}/_{64}$" flat-oval lasher

12" square notched handle with hand hold

Stephen Kostyshyn, *Covered Vessel*, clay, wood, reed, 24"H x 11"W x 10"D, seven changes of direction on a twill pattern.

Joan Brink, *Guardians of the Four Directions*, rattan, maple, ebony, turquoise heishi beads with pipestone Zoni fetish by Darren Shebola, 14"H x 12"Dia, photo: Eric Swanson.

Continuous Twill

The Contemporary Cat's Head Basket *(see page 92) is an exciting one to create because the shape is determined by the weaver's hands. The basket is woven without the use of a mold. Variations occur through color, size and shape. The shape can be very subtle or highly exaggerated, all determined by the tension of the weaving, the number of rows woven before being upsett, and how soon the shape is pulled in. No two shapes will be exactly alike, which is part of the excitement of this basket. I think you will be surprised at how easy this basket is to make. The process defines the shape.*

The weave of the *Contemporary Cat's Head Basket* is a variation of a twill called the Japanese weave. The pattern of the weave is over two elements and under one element. As a continuous twill, it moves fairly quickly. If a continuous twill is woven in only one direction, the pattern will automatically spiral around the basket and diagonal lines will naturally occur. Add color to the equation, and the spiral will appear more prominent.

Billie Ruth Sudduth, *Contemporary Cat's Head Basket* (variation), 20"H x 15"Dia.

Contemporary Cat's Head Basket

DETERMINING THE STAKES

As with any twill basket, you must first determine the number of stakes or spokes required to create the design. A basic formula is to count the number of elements being woven over and under, in increments, and add four to this number (one for each side of the basket). Since the Japanese weave is over two stakes and under one stake, the total is three and the increments are six, nine, twelve, fifteen and so on. Add four to each of these numbers and you will be able to determine the number of stakes needed for smaller or larger baskets using the two/one twill or Japanese weave. (The mathematics of a twill can actually be quite fascinating and fun.)

PREPARATION

The basket can be woven with dyed or natural reed. The twill pattern is more evident if either the stakes or the weavers are dyed. The basket described (see page 92) has dyed stakes and natural weavers until the last five rows. If dyed materials are used, follow the instructions on the dye packet and adhere to safety guidelines.

> **TIP**
>
> **Save the dye for redyeing the rim after it is carved and adjusted to fit the basket.**

Soak one long piece of natural $^{11}/_{64}$" flat-oval reed. Also soak the dyed stakes, but only briefly.

WEAVING THE BASE

The base is similar to those in the *Colonial Chairside* and the *Shaker*

Billie Ruth Sudduth, variations on the *Contemporary Cat's Head Basket*, (top) *Illusions*, reed, dyed and painted, 12"H x 14"W x 14"D; (middle) 13"H x 16"Dia.; (bottom) 11"H x 13"Dia.

Materials for the Contemporary Cat's Head Basket

7 mm dyed flat-oval reed for the stakes	cut 26 @ 47"
11/64" flat-oval reed for the weavers	2 natural pieces (long)
	2 pieces dyed the same color as the stakes (long)
3/16" flat-oval reed for the weavers	20-25 long pieces
7 mm flat reed for the rim row dyed the same color as the stakes	1 piece approximately 40" long
3/8" flat-oval reed for the rim dyed the same color as the stakes	cut 2 @ 40"
11/64" flat-oval reed for lashing dyed the same color as the stakes	1-2 long pieces

Cat's Head Wall Baskets. It may be helpful to use more than one spoke weight when laying out this base, since the stakes are narrow and more difficult to position. The plaited base is easier to weave if there is a large surface on which to work.

There are 13 vertical stakes and 13 horizontal stakes. The spaces between the stakes should resemble squares (not rectangles). Begin by placing the 13 vertical stakes on the table, flat side facing up and flat-oval side against the table. Weave one horizontal stake over and under the midpoint mark. Weave six stakes above the midpoint mark and six stakes below it.

To prevent the shape from being distorted, weave three stakes above the midpoint mark, turn the basket around, and weave three stakes above the midpoint mark again. Turn the basket, and weave three more stakes. Turn yet again, and weave three more stakes. If all the stakes are woven above or below the midpoint mark at the same time, the stakes have a tendency to pull in too much above the midpoint mark and too little below the midpoint mark.

When all stakes are in place, the base should measure 6" square.

Detail of the twill pattern.

TECHNIQUES FOR WEAVING THE CONTEMPORARY CAT'S HEAD BASKET

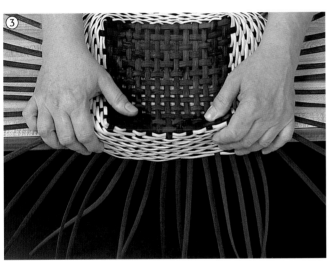

1 Weaving row one before starting the twill pattern.
2 Pulling the corners to the center of the base.
3 Bending the sides.
4 Pushing in the base.
5 Weaving the basket upside down.

Basket at row 65-70 prior to color change.

Changing the color of the weaver at the top of the basket.

Billie Ruth Sudduth, *Contemporary Cat's Head Basket*, dyed reed, twill woven construction, 15"H x 17"W x 17"D.

Patti Quinn Hill, *Guinea Hens*, 100% cotton archival paper, waxed linen, rattan, acrylic paint, 4" to 11"H.

Measure carefully from corner to corner on each side to make sure that this measurement is also 6". For the basket to sit balanced on all four feet, the measurement has to be the same for each corner.

Upsett the Basket

Only the pairs of stakes at each of the four corners are upsett now. Flip the base over so the flat oval side faces up.

Weaving the Sides

Even though the pattern is a twill weave variation, the first row is woven over one stake, under one stake to form a locking row. The weave should be opposite of the base weaver. Since there is not a handle, it does not matter on which side you begin. Taper the end of a piece of $^{11}/_{64}$" flat-oval weaver and insert behind a spoke, flat-oval side facing up. Complete one full revolution around the base. When the starting point is reached, the twill pattern will begin by weaving over two stakes, under one stake, spiraling up the basket. At each row where the starting point is reached, the twill will step one stake to the left. When one long piece of $^{11}/_{64}$" flat-oval weaver runs out, change to $^{3}/_{16}$" flat-oval weaver. Taper the end of the $^{3}/_{16}$" piece so it is the same width as the $^{11}/_{64}$" piece that ran out. This change in the width of the weaver should occur on the same side as the beginning of the basket. This is necessary to keep the basket level at the top.

The Japanese weave is an unbalanced twill, making it more difficult to control the tension. By keeping the middle stake always in the middle, there is less of a tendency to pull too much to the right or to the left. This also helps to keep the base balanced so the basket will sit level on its four feet.

Dona Look, #906, white birch bark, silk thread, woven, stitched, partially wrapped, 7"H x 19¼"W x 4½"D.

SHAPING

Keep the four corners clothespinned together for the first five rows of weaving. At row 1, begin the shaping by fanning the stakes out from each other. As each row is woven, continue fanning out the stakes. Between rows 8 and 12, there should be equal distance between all the stakes. As the corners are rounded, increase the tension on the weaver and pull the corners to the center of the base. By row 15, the feet of the basket should be obvious. Since you are weaving the basket upside down at this stage, the feet will still be the "ears" of the cat.

Between rows 15 and 20, the re-mainder of the basket is upsett. Bend the sides of the basket at the first row of weaving against a table edge. This is the same technique used in Chapter 6 on the *Shaker Cat's Head Wall Basket*. After the edges are creased, pick up the basket and push in on the base with your thumbs. This helps to exaggerate the shape.

Because this is an unbalanced twill, the tension will constantly need to be adjusted and the rows packed down against each other. Do this with the basket right side up, then place it back on the table upside down. Weave another 10 to 15 rows with the basket upside down.

Between rows 25 and 30, the basket will be turned right side up and the weaving continued. At row 35, the stakes should be perpendicular to the base and standing straight up. At row 40, begin to in-crease the tension on the weaver so the stakes will pull in. Keep the space between the stakes even as the tension is increased on each row, pulling the stakes in. Press against the sides as they are being woven to help the corners push out.

Continue the two/one twill until the basket reaches within a couple of inches of the height you want it to be. The basket shown on page 92 has 65 to 70 rows of natural weaver before the color change.

Patti Quinn Hill, *Spirals In and Out*, bread basket, dyed rattan, maple, oak, twill woven, 5"H x 13"Dia.

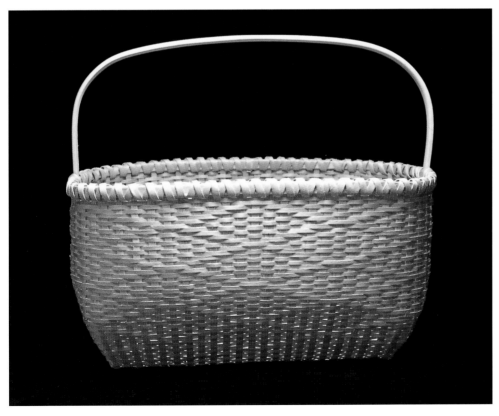

Susi Nuss, *Twilled Carrier*, black ash, mold woven, twill, 9"H x 13"W x 10"D.

Darryl and Karen Arawjo, *Handbags*, hand-split white oak, cane, walnut, cherry, twill woven, 4"H x 6"W x 3"D and 7"H x 9"W x 5"D.

CHANGING COLOR

The top five rows of the basket can be dyed to match the stakes, or they can be left natural. Taper the end of the last piece of natural weaver ($^3/_{16}$" flat-oval) to the same width as the dyed weaver ($^{11}/_{64}$") and insert it as if you were adding a weaver. This should be done on the same side of the basket that row 1 began to keep the basket level at the top. Continue weaving with the dyed reed for five rows. When row 5 ends on the same side of the basket as row 1, taper the dyed weaver to a very narrow taper and weave it over and under the stakes around the basket, losing the weaver on the inside of the basket behind a stake.

ATTACHING A RIM

The top row of weaving will be the rim row, using 7 mm dyed flat reed. It can be woven as a twill, following the spiral design, although it will not show under the rim. Because there are an even number of stakes, at some point the rim row will have to go over and under two stakes.

Bend and tuck the outside stakes to the inside of the basket under the first available row of weaving. Cut the outside stakes even with the top row of weaving.

The rim is $^3/_8$" dyed flat-oval. To give the basket a finished appearance, scarf the overlaps to minimize any bulkiness. After the rim is adjusted to fit the top of the basket and carved, it may need touch-up dyeing.

Lash between every stake. Select a long weaver for the lashing so you will not have to add on a weaver.

In areas where the weaving is loose, tighten with an awl and work back into the basket. "Getting the air out" is necessary on most unbalanced twills.

BALANCE

If the basket remained symmetrical from side to side and the feet are even, the basket should sit level on a flat surface. To make minor adjustments to the feet, push them out from the inside of the basket. If tilted, the basket should also balance on its side without falling.

VARIATIONS

Several other baskets shown in this chapter use the same pattern as the *Contemporary Cat's Head Basket*. Variations occur through size, color, surface embellishment and the addition of a handle. Experiment with this basic twill weave to create your own unique basket, using the *Contemporary Cat's Head* as a guide.

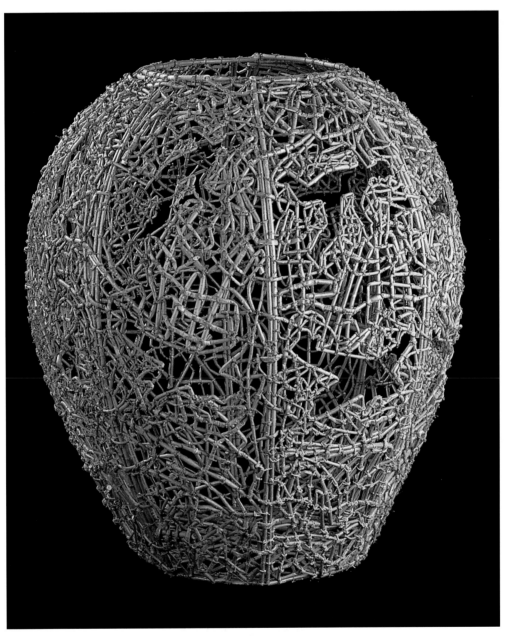

John McQueen, *My Father Turning into A Luscombe*, tied sticks, 25"H x 23"W x 23"D, photo: Russell Johnson.

Ribbed Construction

The classical beauty of the Appalachian Egg Basket *has served as an inspiration for many beginning basketmakers. It uses one of the more difficult woven techniques to master, but the finished product is well worth the effort. As with most baskets, the first two rows of weaving are the most difficult. After two rows, the weaving will hold all the elements in place and the construction will become easier. Read the instructions carefully, and study the demonstration photographs. If your ribs break, take comfort in knowing that every egg basket maker has broken at least one rib.*

Rib baskets have been made in the Central and Southern Appalachian Mountains since the settlers arrived and are still being made today in the time-honored tradition. Oak will probably always be the material of choice for the rib basket because of the beauty and strength of the wood. Identifying the right oak tree and cutting and splitting the oak is an art form in itself. As much skill goes into the preparation of these materials as in the weaving of the basket, and an entirely different set of tools is needed. If you develop an interest in ribbed construction, take the process a step further and learn about splitting oak.

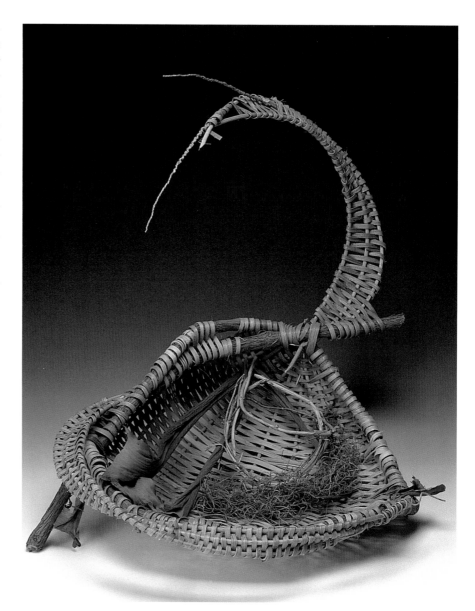

Linda Arter, *Spring*, grapevine, reed, philodendron, inflorescence, ribbed construction, 15"H x 18"D.

There are as many ways of constructing a rib basket as there are nationalities of early settlers. Modern rib baskets are influenced most by German and English techniques. Oak and reed are not the only materials suitable for ribbed construction. The main requirement is that the rib is sturdy. The splits or weavers can be more flexible. As with other types of woven construction, the weave is usually over one and under one.

Appalachian Egg Basket

The *Appalachian Egg Basket* got its name from the purpose for which it was made: to gather eggs from the hen house. It is ridged in the middle to prevent the eggs from rolling against each other and breaking. The shape was developed for it to sit on the hip while gathering eggs or to sit on the back of a horse or mule on the way to market. The egg basket shape is known by many different names which are descriptive of the look and not the function: gizzard, fanny, buttocks, cheek.

Traditional rib baskets require hoops, ears, ribs and weavers. Contemporary rib work requires the same components, but the hoops can be a piece of vine or wood and do not necessarily have to be round or oval; they can be asymmetrical. Regardless of what is used, a frame has to be constructed, and the frame has to be lashed so ribs can be inserted.

PREPARATION

Lightly sand each of the hoops. On hoop one, find the area where the hoop has been joined together. Above that joint on the opposite side of the hoop put an X on the outside. The area with the X will become the handle of the basket.

The exposed handle will have an area measuring 14". Put a pencil mark seven inches down the hoop on each side of the X. This will be the exposed handle area.

The second hoop will become the rim of the basket. It needs to be divided exactly in half. Most 10" hoops measure 32" in circumference. Put a pencil mark at 1 inch and another mark at the halfway point, generally 16 inches. Make adjustments if your hoop measures differently, as each hoop may vary in circumference. Check to see that hoop two is divided exactly in half. The pencil marks are where the two hoops will be lashed together.

PRIMARY AND SECONDARY RIBS

Most egg baskets have primary ribs and secondary ribs. The primary ribs are cut and inserted after the hoops have been lashed together. The secondary ribs are inserted after several rows of weaving have been completed.

Cutting the Primary Ribs

Using #6 round reed, cut the primary ribs as follows:

Rib #1	17"
Rib #2	19"
Rib #3	20"
Rib #4	19"
Rib #5	19"

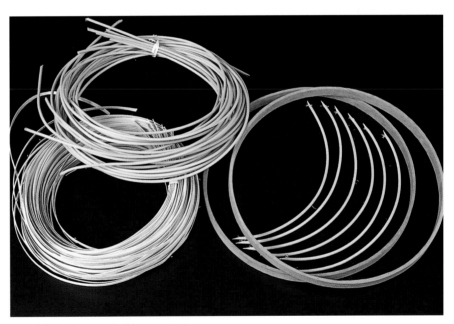

Materials for the *Appalachian Egg Basket*.

Materials for the Appalachian Egg Basket

Two 10-inch hoops

#6 round reed for the ribs

³⁄₁₆" flat reed for the weavers

Cut two sets of these ribs, one for each side of the basket. Whatever is inserted on one side of the basket must also be inserted on the other side to keep the basket symmetrical. Put pencil marks on the middle of the rib to keep the rib placement straight: I, II, III, IIII, etc. Sharpen the ends of the rib to a point. After sharpening each set of ribs, check to see that they are still equal in length.

The better the point you have, the more likely the ribs will stay in place. Do not be concerned if as much as an inch is sharpened off. The measurements allow for this.

Cutting the Secondary Ribs

Next, cut the first set of secondary ribs (two of each):

Rib #1	$12^1/_2$"
Rib #2	13"
Rib #3	$17^1/_2$"
Rib #4	20"
Rib #5	19"
Rib #6	17"
Rib #7	15"

The ribs are numbered to show the order of placement. Sharpen these, then set them aside.

The other set of secondary ribs has only three sizes (cut two of each):

Rib #1	8"
Rib #2	12"
Rib #3	10"

Cut, sharpen, and set aside this set of secondary ribs. The middle rib in each set is cut the longest to give the basket a more pronounced "fanny" shape.

EAR VARIATIONS

The lashing of the two hoops, called an *ear*, may be a simple binding like an X or a more elabo-

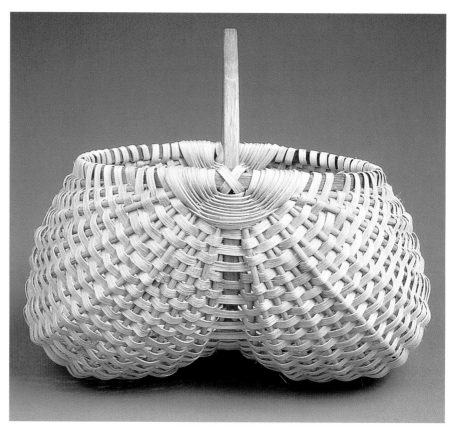

Billie Ruth Sudduth, *Appalachian Egg Basket*, reed, oak, 12"H x 15"W x 10"D.

Three-point lashing.

Sheila King, *Earth Fibers*, grapevine, phylo sheaths, palm fronds, reed, ribbed construction, 20"H x 18"W x 16"D.

rate design. Some of the more traditional ears are the bow knot and the God's Eye, both four-point lashing. The three-point lashing used in this project was widely used in southern Appalachia. It is also known as *donkey's ears*. An advantage of the three-point lashing is that it forms pockets for the ribs to fit in until they are secured by the weaving.

Insert the rim hoop inside the handle hoop, lining up the pencil marks. The X should be visible at the top.

The handle hoop always goes on the outside of the rim hoop.

Wet at least a six-to-eight-foot piece of $^3/_{16}$" flat weaver to lash with—it is very difficult to add lashing on and secure it. The smooth or good side of the weaver should be facing out when beginning the ear.

Three-Point Lashing

1. The end of the weaver goes behind the intersected hoops from the top left to the lower right, rough side against the basket. Leave a small end or tail visible. This can be used later to sign the basket.
2. The weaver passes diagonally on the outside from the top left to the lower right, forming half of an X.
3. The weaver then goes behind the base hoop below the rim and will be positioned on the lower left.

Cynthia W. Taylor, hand-split white oak egg basket with converging ribbing and braid, 10"H x 11"W x 11"D. Ribwork inspired by Central Appalachian traditions.

4. The weaver crosses diagonally from the lower left to the upper right and diagonally back again. An X will be visible on the inside and the outside where the hoops intersect.

5. The weaver moves from the lower left, crosses to the right beneath the rim and goes behind the rim on the right.

6. Next the weaver passes over the rim behind the base hoop and out to the lower left, over the rim. This will complete one full lashing.

Continue by lashing seven more times for a total of eight. Eight lashings are recommended to form deep pockets for the ribs to fit in.

This sounds more complicated than it is. The weaver goes from behind the left rim, over the base hoop, behind the right rim; up and over the right rim, behind the base hoop, and up and over the left rim, etc. Once the first lashing is correct, the others will fall into place. An ear should be formed on each side of the basket.

Do not cut the weaver. You will continue weaving with it after the primary ribs are inserted.

INSERTING THE PRIMARY RIBS

Ribs 1 and 2 go in the pocket underneath the rim. Ribs 4 and 5 go in the pocket along the hoop at the base. To prevent ribs from popping out, insert 1, 2, 4, and 5 on each side of the basket before inserting rib 3. Using an awl, make a hole in the seam where the lashing crosses back and forth. Rib 3 will be inserted in this hole. This is the rib most likely to fall out since it does not have a pocket to fit in.

To secure the ribs in place, weave two rows on one side of the basket, then two rows on the other

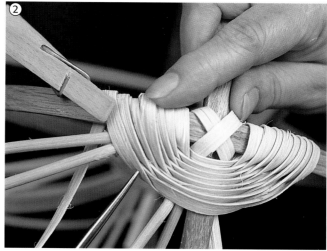

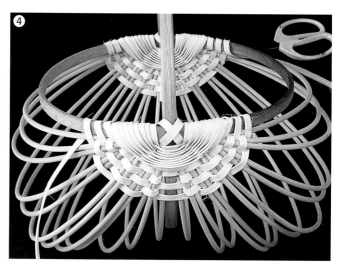

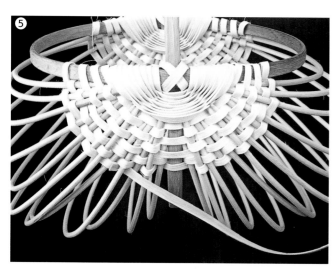

1 Inserting ribs 1, 2, 4, 5.
2 Making a space for rib 3.
3 Placement of primary ribs.
4 First set of secondary ribs inserted.
5 Second set of secondary ribs inserted.
6 Filling in.

Side of basket completely filled in.

side before continuing to weave any further. As with other plaited baskets, the weaving pattern is over one, under one. When moving in one direction, the smooth side of the weaver will be facing the outside, but moving in the other direction, the rough side will be facing out.

To help control the tension and to keep the ribs evenly spaced, weave a few rows on one side of the basket and then a few on the other, rather than all on one side until the weaver runs out. When a weaver does run out, insert the new weaver on top of the existing weaver for two or three ribs and continue weaving. It is almost impossible to hide the ends on a rib basket.

INSERTING SECONDARY RIBS

After five rows are woven on each side of the basket, insert the first set of secondary ribs.

TIP

Make sure your weaver is long enough to complete at least two more rows before needing to add a new weaver.

Rib 1 will be inserted in the space directly below the rim; ribs 2 to 6 will be inserted in the same space as the existing ribs 1 to 5, and rib 7 will be inserted in the space along the bottom hoop. Make sure that seven ribs are inserted on each side of the basket. These secondary ribs should have a measurement somewhere between the lengths of the existing primary ribs which they are placed between. (Secondary rib 1 will be longer than primary rib 1, but shorter than primary rib 2, and so on.) The basket will fan out from rib 1 to rib 3, then gradually go back in toward the base hoop with the remaining ribs.

Continue the weaving pattern of over and under on each side of the basket. Since additional ribs were inserted, the weaving pattern may be interrupted for one row only where two overs and two unders will be side by side. This is normal if it only occurs on one row.

Weave a total of fifteen rows before inserting the final set of sec-

Aaron Yakim, hand-split white oak coal basket, 8"H x 15"W x 15"D, photo: Cynthia W. Taylor. Ribwork inspired by Central Appalachian traditions.

Molly Gardner, *Sierra*, manzanita, willow, ribbed construction, 10"H x 25"W x 14"D, photo: Sonnia Gore.

ondary ribs. Rib 1 will go below the rim, rib 2 below the existing rib 3, and rib 3 along the hoop at the base. At this point, there should be 15 ribs on each side of the basket.

SHAPING

The tension of the weave influences the shape as well as the position of the ribs. Together, the tension of the weave and the position of the ribs determine the shape of the basket. If the ribs are pulled upward and the basket is woven more tightly, there will be a less distinct fanny shape. If the ribs are pushed down toward the base hoop, a more distinct shape will develop. The position of the original rib 3 also greatly affects the shape. The closer to the base this rib is positioned, the more the fanny shape will develop.

Although exact measurements were given for the lengths of primary and secondary ribs, it is likely that several rib lengths will have to be adjusted. This is done by pushing the secondary ribs further into the basket or pulling them further out. The primary ribs should serve as a guide for the remainder of the ribs' positions and lengths. Remember whatever is done on one side of the basket also has to be done on the other side for the basket to remain symmetrical and for the basket to sit flat upon completion.

After all the secondary ribs are in place, the basket should be placed on a flat surface to adjust rib lengths for the basket to sit flat. This should also be done frequently during the weaving of the basket.

FILLING IN

The area around the top rim and the base hoop will likely be woven before the rest of the basket. When this happens, drop down to the next rib and continue as if this were the rim. The last areas to be completed will be between ribs 2, 3 and 4. To keep the weaving equal on each side of the basket, fill in this last area from side to side, rather than all on one side.

On very large rib baskets, there is such a difference in the space between the rim and base hoop that a *gusset* has to be inserted. This is a piece of weaver woven from the middle of one side across to the other side, creating two additional weavers for a total of four weavers going at once. The weaving is done from the ears to the middle of the basket—as well as the middle of the basket toward the ears—on each side. A gusset is not needed on a 10-inch basket.

Left: Vicki Johnson, contemporary oval-ribbed basket, oak, dyed reed, arrow twine, ribbed construction, 5"H x 16"W x 8"D, photo: LSN Studios.

Below: Veronica Stewart, untitled basket, wisteria, vine rattan, pine bark, maple seed pod, ribbed construction, 13"H x 10"W, photo: Jerry Anthony.

TIP

If the basket does not sit level, dampen it slightly and press against the ribs from the inside of the basket. The ribs can be manipulated to balance the basket.

Sharon Algozer, *Interconnections 1*, dyed reed, yucca, ribbed construction, 14"H x 48"W x 20"D, photo: Michael Honer.

Trevle Wood, *Butterfly Basket*, dyed split oak, ribbed construction, 7"H x 6"Dia. Ms. Wood is a fourth-generation white oak basketmaker.

Surface Embellishments

11

Surface embellishments are additions made to baskets once they are complete. They are not essential for the construction of the basket or for the integrity of the design. They are used to add visual interest and change the appearance of a basket. Through the use of surface embellishments, a rather ordinary basket can be transformed into a work of art. There are really no rights or wrongs in this area, so be creative and experiment with adding your own special touch to the baskets you create. Small areas of a basket or the entire piece can be embellished. Twist and turn your reeds, add paint or overlays, or try adding attachments to the baskets. The possibilities are endless.

Wedding Basket

This basket obtained its name from its appearance. The decorative curls suggest a festive occasion to be celebrated, hence the name *Wedding Basket*. It can be filled with gifts or good wishes. The basket is a simple market-type basket constructed like the *Colonial Chairside Basket* in Chapter 5. The decorative handle and curls take it beyond the ordinary.

Susi Nuss, *Matyia Market*, black ash, hickory, mold woven, 10"H x 9"W x 7"D.

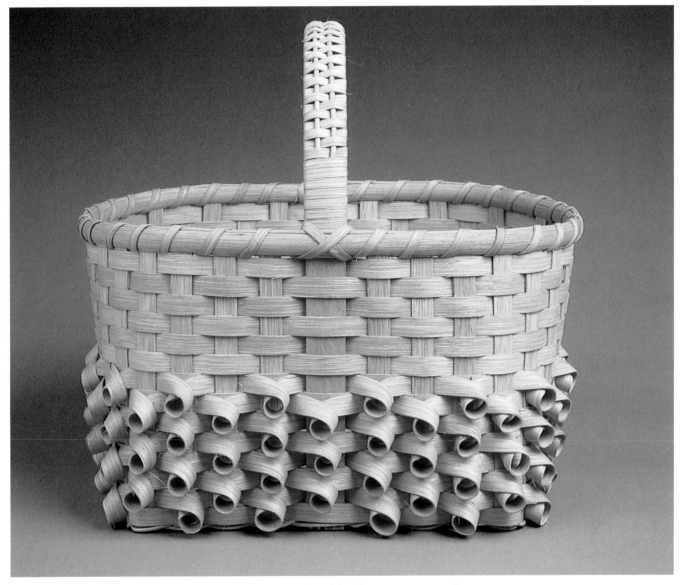

Billie Ruth Sudduth, *Wedding Basket,* plaited with curls, dyed reed, oak handle, 14"H x 12"W x 10"D.

Materials for the Wedding Basket

10" x 14"D handle

⅝" flat reed for stakes (cut 17 @ 36")

½" flat reed for weavers and curls

¼" flat reed for lashing and handle wrap

⅝" flat-oval reed for rim

#2 round reed for twining the base

#6 round reed for the rim filler and handle

WEAVING THE BASE

Place nine stakes lengthwise side by side, ½" apart, lining up the midpoint marks. Weave four stakes to the left of the midpoint, spacing ½" apart, using a plain weave. Weave the handle in along the midpoint lines. Weave the remaining four stakes to the right of the handle. Adjust the base to measure 12"W x 10"D. Twine around the base with the #2 round reed. Upsett the basket.

WEAVING THE SIDES

Weave 13 to 15 rows of ¹/₂" flat reed, using the stop/start method of weaving. Refer to Chapter 5 and the instructions for the *Colonial Chairside Basket*. Do not pack the rows together as tightly as in other baskets. This will allow space to insert the curls later. When the top row is complete, bend the outside stakes to the inside and tuck under the third row of weaving. Cut the inside stakes even with the top row.

HANDLE WRAP

Lay two pieces of #6 round reed across the exposed handle and tuck inside the first row of weaving on one side. Insert the end of a long

TECHNIQUES FOR WEAVING THE WEDDING BASKET

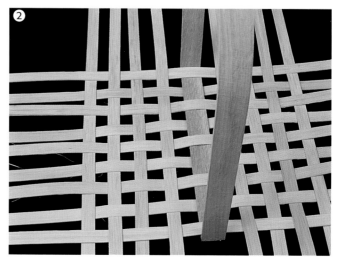

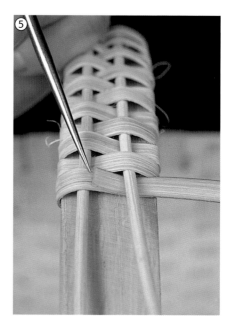

piece of $^1/_4$" flat reed under a tucked stake to secure it; then bind or wrap the handle for eight wraps. Pull tightly on the weaver so that it won't be too loose when it dries. Weave over and under, then under and over, the #6 round reed to the other side of the handle. When you are two inches away from the other side, solid wrap or bind again. Place this loose end under the top row of weaving where a stake is tucked.

TIP

If your weaver runs out while wrapping the handle, lay the end of a new piece on top of the existing weaver and secure the ends underneath the #6 round reed.

RIM

Lay a piece of $^5/_8$" flat-oval reed around the inside and outside top row of weaving, leaving a $^1/_2$" overlap. Place a piece of #6 round reed on top of the rim pieces, butting the ends slightly off center at the handle. Secure in place with clothespins. Lash the rim with $^1/_4$"

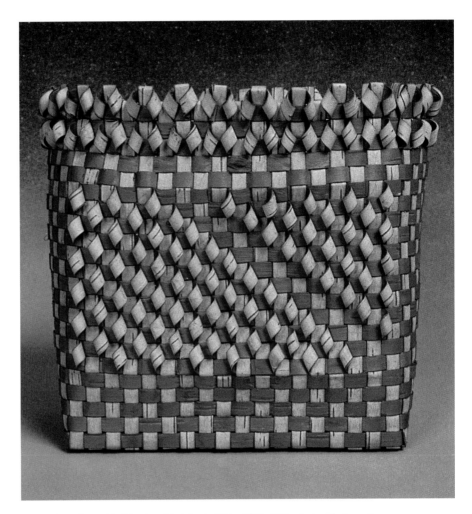

Cass Schorsch, untitled basket, birch bark, 6"H x 7"W x 2"D, photo: Photogenics.

TECHNIQUES FOR WEAVING THE WEDDING BASKET

1 Inserting the handle.
2 Woven base with handle.
3 #6 round reed inserted over the handle.
4 Wrapping the handle.
5 Adding weaver to the handle wrap.
6 Beginning the first curl.
7 Pulling weaver for the second curl.

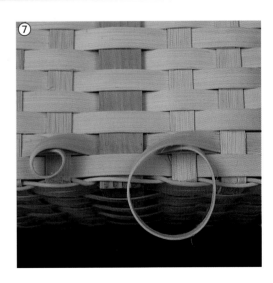

flat reed, making an X at the handle to secure it.

The base can be filled in with $1/2$" or $5/8$" flat-reed scraps. Refer to Chapter 3 for variations on filling in a base.

CURLS

Curls can be added anywhere on the basket after it is complete. The *Wedding Basket* uses seven rows of curls.

Start the curls on the second row of weaving from the base. Tuck the end of a $1/2$" piece of flat reed under a stake on the right, good side facing out. Moving from right to left, curl the reed around your finger, continuing to keep the good side of the reed facing to the outside. Take the end of the reed over the curl and insert under the next stake to the left and then pull it through. Repeat this step moving around the basket.

When the starting curl is reached, tuck the end under the starting stake. A new piece of reed is added by tucking the ending piece and new piece under the same stake, hiding the ends. If you are having difficulty inserting curls, use reed the next size smaller ($3/8$") than the row in which you are inserting them ($1/2$").

A single row of curls can be added or the basket can be completely covered with curls, making it a double-wall basket. A design of curls can be woven on each side in a contrasting color.

The dimensions for the completed *Wedding Basket* are 14"H x 12"W x 10"D.

Sheila M. King, *Tribute to Mother Nature*, round reed, handmade paper, birch bark vines and palm fronds, 12" x 18" x 6".

Bonne Jean Bertlshofer, *Woven Wave*, 21H" x 10"W x 19"D.

Billie Ruth Sudduth, *Appalachian Springs*, dyed flat and round reed, 17"H x 20"W x 14"D.

ROUND REED CONFETTI

Confetti refers to curls made out of round reed. Secure the end of a long piece of round reed to a dowel with a clothespin. Make sure the reed is very wet and pliable so it won't break. Solid wrap or bind the dowel with the round reed until it runs out and secure this second end with a clothespin. Let the reed completely dry before removing the clothespins. The ends of the confetti are woven into the basket and usually show on the inside, adding another decorative dimension. This is a time-consuming process which can totally transform the appearance of a basket.

This type of curl is affected by humidity. It can be sprayed with a polyurethane matte spray to keep the tension in the curl tight.

OVERLAYS

An overlay is weaving over existing weaving, usually using a contrasting color. This decorative accent can draw attention to features such as basket signatures, corners, or twill patterns. It is an easy technique to use but does require some patience in hiding the ends of the weavers.

If the weaving is unusually tight, it can be difficult to add overlays. It is easier if the basket is completely dry and the weaver only slightly damp. The advantages of an overlay are that it highlights design and allows color to be put right where you want it.

PAINTING ON BASKETS

This embellishment offers the widest range of possibilities. A design can be painted only on the rim

Judy Dominic, *Earth Mother Series #5*, gourd, waxed linen, various muds, knotless netting, modified bogolan "fini," 6"H x 5½"Dia, photo: Chuck Schauer.

Carole Hetzel and Steven Hetzel, reed and copper, 19"H x 11"W x 13"D.

or can be painted over the entire surface of the basket. One color can be used or a rainbow of colors. Before any painting is done, the basket fibers have to be sealed or the paint will spread and penetrate the fibers. A polyurethane matte spray works well to seal the fibers. It is lightly sprayed on the surface of the basket and dries quickly.

TIP

To paint small designs on a basket, cut off the bristles of the paint brush and use the metal tip for painting. This prevents a buildup of paint on bristles and makes controlling the amount of paint easier.

Billie Ruth Sudduth, *Signature Basket*, dyed reed with stained overlay, continuous plaiting, 8"H x 8"W x 8"D.

Billie Ruth Sudduth, *Speculation*, dyed and painted reed, twill weave, 14"H x 16"W x 16"D.

STENCILING

Since stenciling uses a smaller amount of paint, sealing the basket fibers is usually not necessary. Decades ago, a cut potato was used to stamp or stencil a basket. A design was carved in the end of the cut potato, then dipped into paint and stamped on the basket.

WHITEWASHING

After the basket is complete, a very diluted coat of paint can be brushed on the basket. Whitewashing gives the basket an aged look. Water-based paint is preferable for this technique.

ATTACHMENTS

Almost any item can be attached to a basket by gluing, stitching, wrapping, or weaving. The most common attachments are beads, feathers, shells, bells, buttons, yarns and metal.

Painting the basket rim.

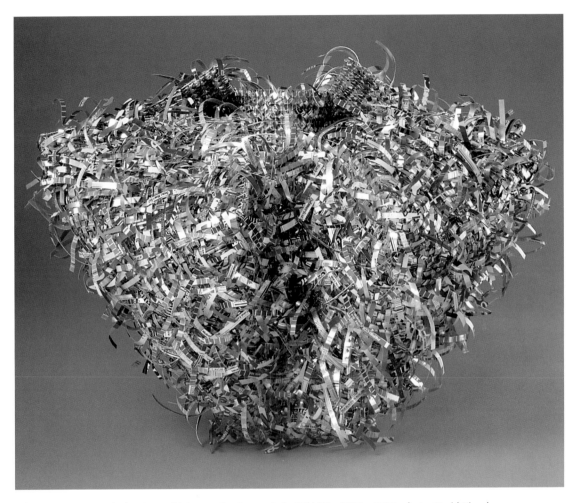

John Garrett, *Pop Pod*, aluminum drink cans, hardware cloth, 13½"H x 19"W x 19"D, photo: David Kingsbury.

Non-Woven Construction

Baskets is a very broad term that encompasses all sorts of images. A basket is a vessel, it is a container, it is a carrier, it is a familiar object. Basketry crosses craft mediums in that potters, glass blowers, paper makers and metalsmiths make objects they call baskets. Basketry is one of the few craft mediums that is identifiable by the technique and not by the material. The common bond is that the object, whether functional or sculptural, is woven, plaited, twined, ribbed or coiled.

Most baskets fit within these parameters, but a few do not. Contemporary basketmakers are exploring various techniques, some new, some borrowed from other media, and are experimenting with a variety of materials to create an entirely new definition of a basket. The results are exciting and are pushing the limits of this timeless object.

Coils, Stitches, and Knots

The following represent some of the more popular or innovative non-woven construction techniques in present-day basketry. While these descriptions should give you an idea of the variety available, they are far from exhaustive. I strongly encourage those in-

Elizabeth Whyte Schulze, *Bull and Horses*, raffia, reed, acrylic paint, coiled, 20½"H x 19½"Dia.

terested to find out more about these baskets (and perhaps to write about them, as this area is in need of an in-depth treatment that cannot possibly be provided here).

COILED

The techniques used to coil a basket are usually identified with sewing, rather than with weaving. Coiling itself is a sewing, not a weaving, technique, so there is no warp or weft. Instead, the two components to a coiled basket are: the *foundation* or the *core*, and the sewing material. The foundation or core is usually a hard material, and the sewing or stitching material is softer and more pliable.

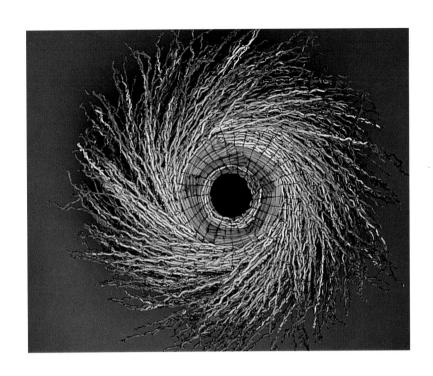

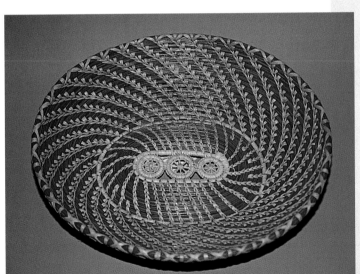

Top: Kathleen Peelen Krebs, *Oasis Bloom*, pine needles, date palm inflorescence, waxed linen, coiled, 8"H x 15"Dia, photo: G. Krebs.

Above: B. Lee Sipe, untitled basket, pine needles, raffia, coiled, 5"H x 16"Dia.

Right: Joanna Lindsly, *Westward*, coiled raffia over reed, acrylic paint, dye, embroidery floss, laser copies of art, 11¼"H x 7"Dia, photo: Tom Moulin.

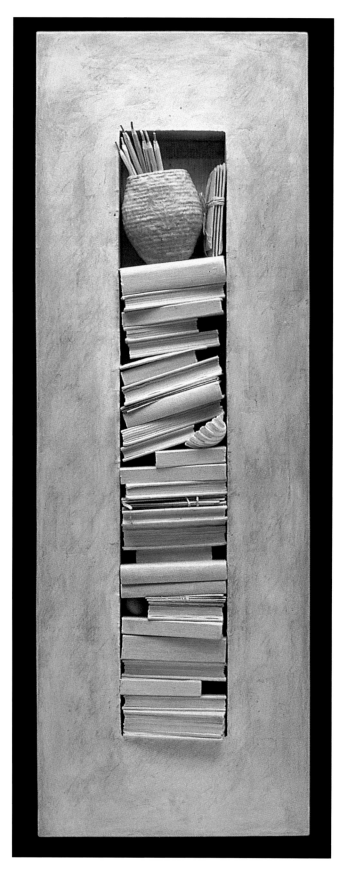

Lissa Hunter,
So Little Time,
wood, paper, hemp
cord, raffia, forsythia
sticks, leaf, found
objects, paint,
spackling, graphite,
coiled basket,
40"H x 14"W x
3½"D,
photo: K.B. Pilcher.

Most coiled baskets are round or oval, beginning with a center core. The core is wrapped as the coils are stacked and stitched to form the basket. A bone awl, needle, or the blunt end of a teaspoon (as with Gullah baskets) is often used to create the stitches. Because the coiling is tightly stitched, the baskets are usually quite sturdy, somewhat rigid, and durable. The simplest of the coiled baskets are wrapped and stitched. More complex coiled baskets use a variety of stitches, the figure-of-eight being more complicated than the wrap-and-stitch.

Coiled baskets can be the most laborious of all basket techniques because of the number of stitches to the inch. Generally, the more stitches to the inch, the finer the coiling. Materials suitable for the core include cordage such as rope, bundles of grasses, seagrass, straws, jute, sisal and rush. Stitching materials include raffia, finely split cane, willow skein, palmetto leaf, string and wax linen. The choices are endless. Coiled baskets are often embellished with other natural materials, found objects and paint.

Basic coiling stitches for interlacing are:
- Figure-of-eight or Navajo stitch
- Oversew
- Lazy "S" stitch

Left: Linda Fifield, *Forest Fire*, glass beads, nylon thread, wooden vessel, netting stitch, 6½"H x 4½"Dia.

Below: Katherine Westphal, *Sun Dance*.

Linda Fifield, *Totems*, nylon thread, glass beads, wooden vessel, netting, 7"H x 2¾"Dia.

Native American coiled baskets, particularly those found in the southwestern parts of the United States, are some of the most beautiful and sought-after baskets on the planet. The names for many of the stitches associated with coiling are attributable to them.

KNOTTED

An application taken from fiber and textile techniques is knotless netting. With the resurgence of the popularity of basketmaking in the 1980s, knotting has come into prominence as a major basket technique. However, references to knotting are most often found in books on macramé, not books on basketry.

This form of basketry yields small vessels that are sculptural, colorful, and designed to hold your interest. The technique is as laborious as coiling and requires a great deal of patience, but the possibilities of design are quite vast. Wax linen is frequently used in the con-

Kate Anderson,
Andy Warhol Cup,
knotted waxed linen,
plastic Coke
bottles handle,
5"H x 6¾"Dia,
photo: David Kingsbury.

struction, offering a rainbow of color possibilities. Other materials suitable for knotting include thread, rope, raffia and string. Knotting allows a rich range of patterns as well.

Knotting is more than just tying knots. In fact, it is more like looping than actual knotting. In thinking of knotting, imagine tying shoelaces. The tension on each side of the knot is equal. In knotting, the tension of the two elements is not equal. One thread travels inside the loop being made, and the other thread actually forms the loop. One thread is the core, similar to coiling, and is inactive or passive. The

Norman Sherfield, *Honey Dipper*, knotted waxed linen and stones, 3"H x 10"W x 3"D.

other thread or threads are active and make a loop over the passive thread and are pulled tightly.

The basic knots in knotting are: the lark's head, the half hitch, and the full hitch. Macramé books are a good source of information on these and other stitches.

The components of knotting include:

- Ribs—the rows made by the knotting stitch.
- Fabric—the flat or three-dimensional surface created by the rows of knotting.
- Elements—the materials used to make the core or knot.

The process is time consuming and the materials small, but the finished product is well worth the effort.

STITCHED

Contemporary basketmakers use a variety of stitching techniques to create their baskets. Many of these techniques are borrowed from other mediums such as embroidery, needlepoint, crochet and knitting. Some baskets are woven off-loom with a gourd or peyote stitch.

In constructing beaded baskets, a needle and thread is used to connect the beads to each other one bead at a time, forming a fabric of glass beads and nylon thread. The stitch, sometimes known as a twill stitch or diagonal weave, is a netting technique. The bead replaces the knot in a net structure. The stitch can be self-supporting or worked over a form or mold. The beads are more than embellishments. They are the actual walls of the basket.

WRAPPED

Wrapped baskets use many of the techniques from coiled baskets but do not include stitching. The mate-

Patsy K. Walden, *Crescent Moon*, coiled pine needles, artificial sinew, clay sphere, 11"H x 10"W x 6"D.

Ruth Greenberg, *Pitcher II*, bindweed, driftwood, knotless netting, 2.7"H x 2.7"W x 3"D, photo: Phillips Camera.

Ann Hall-Richards, *Swelling Consciousness*, cast paper, twined waxed linen, 12"H x 18"W x 5"D, photo: Warwick Green Photography.

rials are joined in some other manner, such as with glue or rivets. A hard core can be continuously wrapped around itself, spiraling out from the center, creating spaces between the materials. Since stitching and weaving are not involved, a separate base has to be constructed to attach and secure the basket form.

CAST AND MOLDED

Paper or fabric is used to cast or mold a basket. Handmade paper sheets from junk mail and dryer lint are layered over a form such as a bowl or glass jar. The wet paper is glued with wallpaper paste as it is layered around the form and fabric is added. While wet, feet may be inserted or other embellishments added.

Objects of any shape can be used to cast or mold a basket. The only requirement is that the mold not be porous, or it will absorb the water and paste as the basket is being layered. The top of the basket must also be wide enough to remove the mold.

Other techniques include folding a form and stitching or riveting embellishments to the pre-made form. Embroidered fabric is heavily starched, layered over a form, and allowed to dry. The completed object resembles a basket.

• • •

The definition of a basket has greatly expanded over the past 25 years. Today, the techniques, styles, sizes, colors and materials are as varied as the makers themselves. This object called a basket is an art form of incredible variety and timeless beauty.

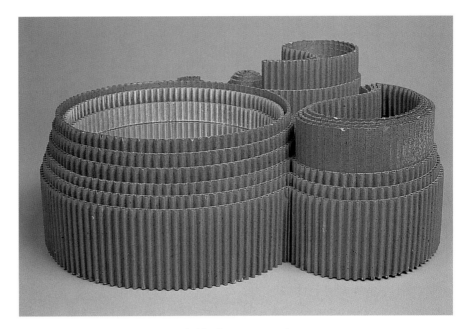

Charles Dowd, Kate Groff Dees, untitled baskets, corrugated paper.

Mary Ruth Webb, untitled basket, handmade paper, fabric, bamboo, 12"H x 8"W x 8"D.

Norma Minkowitz, *Floater*, crochet, fiber, paint, 15$\frac{1}{2}$"H x 12$\frac{1}{2}$"W x 12$\frac{1}{2}$"D, collection: Karen Mesch Beatty, photo: Bobby Hansson.

Appendices

Jane Sauer, *No Separation*, waxed linen thread and paint, knotting, 27½"H x 16"W x 10"D, photo: David Kingsbury.

Appendix A
Glossary

Add on. Add a new weaver to the existing weaver.

Awl. A pointed tool used to punch a hole in a three-point lashing for rib placement or to open up spaces in the weaving.

Balanced twill. A weave in which the number of elements woven over and under are the same.

Base. The bottom of the basket.

Bend and tuck. The technique of ending and securing the stakes or spokes before the rim is attached.

Butt. Ends of weaving material placed flush against each other.

Chase weave. A weaving technique using two pieces of weaver at the same time, one making a full revolution, and the second weaver "chasing" the first around the basket.

Coil. A pound of weaver tied in a circle.

Coiling. A technique of basketry where a core is wrapped and then stitched as the core is stacked and layered.

Continuous weave. Weaving a basket continuously until the weaver ends and a new weaver is added.

Curls. An Algonquin technique used to embellish baskets.

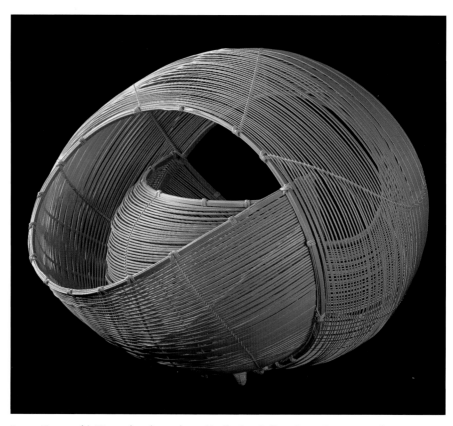

Ryuun Yamaguchi, *Waves*, bamboo, photo: Textile Arts Gallery, Santa Fe, New Mexico.

Depth. The measurement across the basket from front to back.

Diagonal weave. A technique of weaving where the base and sides interweave with themselves to form the basket.

Double bottom. A base construction where base two is placed on top of base one and woven in place.

Dyeing. The method of adding natural or chemical color to the weaving material.

Ear. The area where the hoops of a rib basket are joined.

Embellishments. Decorative features added to a basket.

Fanny. A term used to describe the symmetrical base of a rib basket on each side of the base hoop. Also known as *gizzard* or *buttocks*.

Filler. The material used to fill in spaces in a basket.

Filling in. Completing a rib basket between the rim and base hoops. Also a technique of closing the base of a basket.

Handle. The area of the basket used for carrying.

Height. The measurement referring to how tall the basket is from the base to the top.

Hoops. The round, oval, or square frame of rib baskets which are lashed together.

Japanese weave. Weaving which goes over two elements and under one in a spiral pattern.

Lash. Bind.

Lashing. The technique of binding rims together.

Losing a weaver. A technique of hiding the end of a weaver to keep it from being visible.

Notch. The carved-out area on the handle where the rim is inserted to secure it in place.

Overlap. Laying one weaver beside or on top of another and then weaving as one.

Overlays. Weaving color over the top of existing weaving.

Packing. Pushing each row of weaving securely against the row beneath it.

Plain weave. An over-and-under weave.

Plaited. Woven.

Norman D. Sherfield, *High Rise*, knotted wax linen, found objects, 25"H x 2¹/₂"W x 2¹/₂"D, photo: David Kingsbury.

Patti Lechman, *Eos,* knotted nylon, 5"H x 6"W x 5"D.

John Garrett, *Winged Chronicle*, engraved copper, rivets, 15"H x 20"W x 20"D, photo: David Kingsbury.

Randing. An over-and-under weave using a single weaver, usually referring to round reed woven on an odd number of stakes or spokes.

Rattan. The palm plant which is the source of reed.

Reed. The inner core of the rattan palm plant which is commercially available for basketry.

Reverse. Pattern goes in the opposite direction.

Rib. A technique of basket construction where hoops are lashed together for ribs to be inserted to form the skeleton of the basket.

Rim. The top of the basket along the inside and the outside top row.

Rim filler. Materials placed between the rims to cover the top of the last row of weaving and to add stability to the basket.

Round. One complete weaving revolution around the basket.

Row. One complete revolution of the weaver around the basket.

Scarf. A method of cutting at an angle to join two ends together.

Spiral. Continuously weaving up the sides of a basket in a twill or Japanese weave.

Splints. Strips of weaving materials used for stakes, spokes, and weavers.

Spoke weight. A heavy ruler-like tool used to hold spokes or stakes in place as a basket base is being woven.

Spokes. The elements forming the base of a round basket.

Stain. A color added to a basket which is lighter than the color dye produces.

Stakes. The elements forming the base of a square or rectangular basket.

Stephen Kostyshyn, *Vase*, clay vessel, reed spokes and weavers, 11"H x 10"W x 10"D.

Step up. A term used in twill weaving where each row is started one stake or spoke to the left or right of the previous row.

Taper. Cut at a gradual angle.

Three-point lashing. The technique of interlacing the three hoops of a rib basket.

Three-rod wale. An over two, under one weave with three weavers inserted behind three consecutive spokes and stakes and woven one after the other.

Truing a base. Adjusting the woven base to the exact measurements required.

Twill. Weaving over and under two or more elements at the same time.

Twining. A technique of weaving with two pieces of weaver at the same time, one going in front of and the other behind the same stake or spoke, with a twist in between.

Unbalanced twill. A weave in which the number of elements woven over are not the same as the number of elements woven under.

Undulating. Weaving that has an uneven, wavy appearance.

Upsett. Bending the spokes or stakes over themselves at the base so they will stand upright. Upstake.

Wales. Three or more weavers which twist around each other as they weave over two and behind one spoke.

Warp. The stakes or spokes of a basket.

Weaver. The material used to construct the basket after the base or frame is woven.

Weft. The weavers in a basket.

Width. The measurement at the widest point of the basket.

Appendix B
Suppliers

Allen's Basketworks
11008 SE Main Street
Milwaukie, OR 97222
503-238-6384

Atkinson's Country House
2775 Riniel Road
Lennon, MI 48449
800-832-3071

The Caning Shop
926 Gilman Street
Berkeley, CA 94710
800-544-3373

Carolina Basketry
2703 Hwy. 70 East
New Bern, NC 28560
919-637-6290

Connecticut Cane & Reed Co.
134 Pine Street
Box 762
Manchester, CT 06045
800-227-8498

The Country Seat
1013 Old Philly Pike
Kempton, PA 19529
610-756-6124

Earth Guild
33 Haywood Street
Asheville, NC 28801
800-327-8448

English Basketry Willows
412 Cty Rd 31
Norwich, NY 13815
607-336-9031

Frank's Cane and Rush Supply
7252 Heil Avenue
Huntingdon Beach, CA 92647
714-847-0707

Linda Lugenbill, *XL Round*, wisteria, reed, handspun fibers, dye, rib construction, 36"H x 35"W x 38"D, photo: Rik Helstrom.

Judy Dominic, *Sheltered*, pine branch, dyed rattan reed and cane, drilled, ribbed construction, plain weave, 9"H x 16"W x 7"D, photo: Chuck Schauer.

G.H. Productions
521 E. Walnut Street
Scottsville, KY 42164
800-447-7008

Grandma's Baskets and Supplies
603 S. Putnam
Williamston, MI 48895
800-238-2323

Gratiot Lake Basketry
Star Route 1, Box 16
Mohawk, MI 49950
906-337-5116

H.H. Perkins
10 S. Bradley
Woodbridge, Ct. 06525
800-462-6660

Nate's Nantuckets
171 Eastman Hill Road
Sanbornton, NH 03269
603-286-8927

Ozark Basketry Supply
PO Box 599
Fayetteville, AR 72702
501-442-9292

Plymouth Reed & Cane Supply
1200 W. Ann Arbor Road
Plymouth, MI 48170
313-455-2150

Restoration Products
3191 West 975 South
Fairmount, IN 46928
800-562-5291

Royalwood LTD.
517 Woodville Road
Mansfield, OH 44907
800-526-1630

Suzanne Moore's N.C. Basket Works
130 Main Street
Vass, NC 28394
800-338-4972

W. Cushing and Co.
21 North Street
Kennebunkport, ME 04046
207-967-3711

Woven Spirit Basketry
635 Tamiami Trail North
Nokomis, FL 34275
800-697-6730

Appendix C
Suggested Reading

Trevle Wood, flat-bottom egg basket, split oak, ribbed construction, 10"H x 11"W x 11"D.

GENERAL REFERENCE BOOKS

Appalachian White Oak Basketmaking
Rachel Nash Law and Cynthia W. Taylor
The University of Tennessee Press, Knoxville, TN
1991

A Basketmaker in Rural Japan
Louise Allison Cort and Nakamura Kenji
Smithsonian Institution, Washington, DC
1994

Basketry of the Appalachian Mountains
Sue H. Stephenson
Van Nostrand Reinhold Co., New York, NY
1977

Basketry: The Shaker Tradition
John McGuire
Sterling Publishing Co., Inc., New York, NY
1989

Basketry Today with Materials from Nature
Dona Z. Meilach and Dee Menagh
Crown Publishers Inc., New York, NY
1979

Baskets and Basketmakers in Southern Appalachia
John Rice Irwin
Schiffer Publishing Co., Exton, PA
1982

The Complete Book of Baskets and Basketry
Dorothy Wright
David and Charles Inc., North Pomfret, VT
1983 (First edition 1977)

Contemporary Wicker Basketry
Flo Hoppe
Lark Books, Asheville, NC
1996

Earth Basketry
Osma Gallinger Tod
Crown Publishers, New York, NY
1972

A Modern Approach to Basketry
Dona Meilach
Crown Publishers Inc., New York, NY
1974

The Nature of Basketry
Ed Rossbach
Schiffer Publishing Co., West Chester, PA
1986

Jane Sauer, *Uluru*, knotted waxed linen, 20"H x 13"W x 5½"D, photo: David Kingsbury.

Color Control
B.J. Crawford
An Earth Guild Hand Book
Earth Guild, Asheville, NC
1992

NATIVE AMERICAN BASKETS

Basketmakers: Meaning and Form in Native American Baskets
Edited by Linda Mowat, Howard Morphy and Penny Dransart
Pitt Rivers Museum, University of Oxford, England
1992

Indian Baskets
Sarah Peabody Turnbaugh and William A. Turnbaugh
Schiffer Publishing, West Chester, PA
1986

Weaving New Worlds
Sarah H. Hill
The University of North Carolina Press, Chapel Hill, NC
1997

PATTERN BOOKS

The Basket Book
Lyn Siler
Sterling Publishing Co., Inc., New York, NY
1988

Handmade Baskets
Lyn Siler
Sterling Publishing Co., Inc., New York, NY
1991

Splintwoven Basketry
Robin Taylor Daugherty
Interweave Press, Loveland, CO
1986

Old New England Splint Baskets
John E. McGuire
Schiffer Publishing Co., West Chester, PA
1985

The Techniques of Basketry
Virginia Harvey
University of Washington Press, Seattle, WA
1986

Wicker Basketry
Flo Hoppe
Interweave Press, Loveland, CO
1989

DYEING

Color and Dyeing
Harriet Tidball
Shuttle Craft Monograph Sixteen
HTH Publishers, Santa Ana, CA
1965

Appendix D
Basket Associations and Guilds

UNITED STATES

Many state associations and guilds have local chapters spread throughout their state. Classes, seminars, and conventions are held at various times and locations during the year. Membership is usually a prerequisite for attending. The following organizations are listed alphabetically by state:

Basket Artisans of Arizona
c/o Valerie Bland
4636 E. Stanford Ave.
Higley, AZ 85236
602-830-9366

Arkansas Basketweavers Guild
c/o Laura Hairston
1001 Raven Road
Rogers, AR 72756
501-636-1784

Los Angeles Basketry Guild
c/o Judy Mulford
2098 Mandeville Canyon Road
Los Angeles, CA 90049
310-472-2020

Colorado Basketmakers Guild
c/o Sandy Marsh
8345 Cochise Rd.
Colorado Springs, CO 80908
719-495-0474

Basketweavers Guild of Georgia
PO Box 1309
Roswell, GA 30077
770-475-4323

John Skau, selections from *Forest of Baskets,* tubular plaiting, twill, plain double weave, maple, birch, rosewood, acrylic paint, wood dye, varnish, 67$\frac{1}{2}$" to 83$\frac{1}{2}$"H.

Indiana Basketmakers Association
c/o Elaine Williamson
6803 Rockdale Court
Ft. Wayne, IN 46835
317-881-7747

Iowa Basketmakers Guild
c/o Peggie Wilcox Arends
R.R. 1, Box 36
Stanhope, IA 50246

Northeast Basketmakers Guild
c/o Diane Stanton
365 High Street
Pembroke, MA 02359
617-826-2610

Association of Michigan Basketmakers
c/o Marianne King
48201 Virginia
Macomb, MI 48044
517-772-3069

Missouri Basketweavers Guild
c/o Rhonda Snyder
208 Pilliard Hill Lane
Bismark, MO 63624

Nebraska Basket Weavers Guild
3428 Bline Ave.
Omaha, NE 68123

Great Basin Basketmakers
c/o Mary Lee Fulkerson
4321 Bridle Way
Reno, NV 89509

Basketmakers of New Jersey
c/o Tina Barrows
PO Box 398
Bedminster, PA 18910
215-795-2182

North Carolina Basketmakers Association
c/o Jimmie Kent
1719 Old Folkstone Road
Sneads Ferry, NC 28460
910-337-2528

Columbia Basin Basketry Guild
Multnomah Art Center
7688 SW Capitol Highway
Portland, OR 97219

Upper S.C. Basketmakers Guild
c/o Sandy Elbrecht
504 Tiffany Lane
Taylors, SC 29687
864-292-3845

East Tennessee Basket Association
c/o Susan Sweeter
227 Brushy Valley
Powell, TN 37849
423-938-7627

High Country Basketry Guild
PO Box 167
Annandale, VA 22003

Northwest Basketweavers: Vi Phillips Basketry Guild
PO Box 5657
Lynnwood, WA 98048

AUSTRALIA

Fiber Basketweavers of South Australia
PO Box 646
North Adelaide
South Australia 5006
Australia

CANADA

Basketry Network
c/o Melinda Mayhall
16 Moore Avenue
Toronto M4R IV3
Canada

ENGLAND

Basketmakers Association
c/o Sally Goymer
37 Mendip Road
Cheltenham, Glos GL52 3EB
England

Appendix E

Craft Schools Offering Basketry Classes

Appalachian Center for Crafts
Box 430, Route 3
Smithville, TN 37166

Arrowmont School of Arts and Crafts
PO Box 567
Gatlinburg, TN 37738

John C. Campbell Folk School
One Folk School Road
Brasstown, NC 28902

Haystack Mountain School of Crafts
Deer Isle, ME 04627

Penland School of Crafts
Penland Road
Penland, NC 28765

Peters Valley Craftsmen
19 Kuhn Road
Layton, NJ 07851

Dona Look, *Basket #966*, white birch bark and silk thread, stitched and partially wrapped, 13½"H x 10¾"W x 10¾"D.

Appendix F
Metric Conversion Tables

Metric Conversion

To convert	To	Multiply by
Inches	Centimeters	2.54
Centimeters	Inches	0.40
Feet	Centimeters	30.50
Centimeters	Feet	0.03
Yards	Meters	0.90
Meters	Yards	1.10
Sq. Inches	Sq. Centimeters	6.45
Sq. Centimeters	Sq. Inches	0.16
Sq. Feet	Sq. Meters	0.09
Sq. Meters	Sq. Feet	10.80
Sq. Yards	Sq. Meters	0.08
Sq. Meters	Sq. Yards	1.20
Pounds	Kilograms	0.45
Kilograms	Pounds	2.20
Ounces	Grams	28.40
Grams	Ounces	0.04

Inches to Centimeters

Inches	CM	Inches	CM
1/8	0.3	19	48.3
1/4	0.6	20	50.8
3/8	1.0	21	53.3
1/2	1.3	22	55.9
5/8	1.6	23	58.4
3/4	1.9	24	61.0
7/8	2.2	25	63.5
1	2.5	26	66.0
1 1/4	3.2	27	68.6
1 1/2	3.8	28	71.1
1 3/4	4.4	29	73.7
2	5.1	30	76.2
2 1/2	6.4	31	78.7
3	7.6	32	81.3
3 1/2	8.9	33	83.8
4	10.2	34	86.4
4 1/2	11.4	35	88.9
5	12.7	36	91.4

Appendix G
Contributing Artists

Jackie Abrams
Topsham, VT
Pages 20, 61

Sharon Algozer
Claremont, CA
Pages 19, 108

Kate Anderson
St. Louis, MO
Page 125

Rhonda Anderson
Gray, ME
Page 40

**Darryl and Karen
   Arawjo**
Bushkill, PA
Front cover, 16, 96

Linda Arter
Hammond, LA
Page 98

David Paul Bacharach
Cockeysville, MD
Pages 53, 67

Dorothy Gill Barnes
Worthington, OH
Page 55

Bonne Jean Bertlshofer
Brevard, NC
Page 114

Rowena Bradley
Cherokee, NC
Page 50

Joan Brink
Santa Fe, NM
Page 87

Clay Burnette
Columbia, SC
Front cover, 37

Gail Campbell
Bisbee, AZ
Page 18

Dorothy Chapman
Conehatta Tribal
   Reservation, MS
Page 17

Jill Choate
Talkeetna, AK
Page 39

Kathleen Dalton
Tellico Plains, TN
Page 6

Jayne Hare Dane
Heath, MA
Page 24

Michael Davis
Roswell, GA
Page 33

Kate Groff Dees
Tarpon Springs, FL
Page 127

Judy A. Dominic
Harrison, OH
Pages 116, 135

Charlie Dowd
Bakersville, NC
Page 127

Fred Ely
Interlochen, MI
Page 56

Linda Farve
Philadelphia, MS
Page 17

Linda Fifield
McKee, KY
Pages 123, 124

Mary Lee Fulkerson
Reno, NV
Page 15

Dan Gable
Maitland, FL
Page 15

Bonnie Gale
Norwich, NY
Page 12

Molly Gardner
Sun Valley, NV
Page 106

John Garrett
Albuquerque, NM
Pages 119, 132

Elizabeth Geisler
Sarasota, FL
Page 31

Ruth Greenberg
Trinidad, CA
Page 126

Herman Guetersloh
Houston, TX
Front cover, 43

Ann Hall-Richards
Minneapolis, MN
Pages 77, 126

Johanna Heller
Hammond, LA
Page 62

**Carole and Steven
   Hetzel**
West Palm Beach, FL
Page 116

Patti Quinn Hill
Weaverville, NC
Front cover, 41, 93, 95

Bryant Holsenbach
Durham, NC
Page 11

Lissa Hunter
Portland, ME
Page 122

Ferne Jacobs
Los Angeles, CA
Page 23

Vicki Johnson
Sparks, NV
Page 107

Soho Katsushiro
Kanto Region, Japan
Page 85

Jimmie Kent
Sneads Ferry, NC
Page 80

Sheila M. King
Gladwin, MI
Pages 40, 101, 114

Sue Kolvereid
Berwyn, PA
Page 75

Stephen Kostyshyn
Bellaire, MI
Pages 86, 133

Kathleen Peelen Krebs
Berkeley, CA
Page 121

**Marion and Arthur
   Landfors**
Needham, MA
Page 65

Patti Lechman
Memphis, TN
Pages 7, 131

Jin Morigami, untitled basket, bamboo, photo: Textile Arts Gallery, Santa Fe, New Mexico.

Index